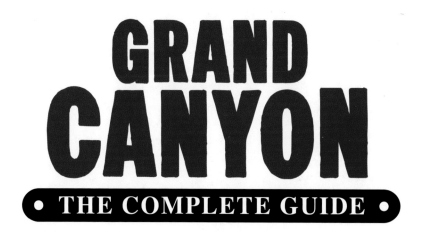

GRAND CANYON

• THE COMPLETE GUIDE •

3rd Edition

WINNER
(1st Edition)

Benjamin Franklin Award
Best Full-Color Travel Guide

Independent Publisher Book Award
Best Travel Guide

W9-BON-134

JAMES KAISER

CONTENTS

ADVENTURES (p.19)

Hiking, river rafting, mule rides, scenic flights—Grand Canyon has it all! The only question is what not to do in the park.

GEOLOGY (p.33)

Learn about the powerful forces that shaped Grand Canyon, exposing nearly two billion years of Earth history.

ECOLOGY (p.43)

Far from being a desolate wasteland, Grand Canyon is home to an amazing range of plants and animals that coexist in remarkable ways.

WILDLIFE (p.48)

Many fascinating animals call Grand Canyon home, including rattlesnakes, mountain lions, bobcats, bighorn sheep, and the California condor.

HISTORY (p.69)

Over the past 10,000 years, Grand Canyon has been home to both prehistoric cultures and modern Indian tribes. Discovered by Coronado in 1540, the Canyon was avoided by settlers for hundreds of years. In 1869 John Wesley Powell became the first man to run the Colorado River in Grand Canyon, a remarkable adventure that paved the way for further exploration. More recently, Grand Canyon has been center stage for some of the most contentious environmental battles in America.

The South Rim (p.107)

The most famous and popular part of Grand Canyon—home to nearly two dozen easily accessible viewpoints. Stay at a historic lodge, dine on a gourmet meal, or simply take in the breathtaking views.

The North Rim (p.253)

Wild and remote, the North Rim combines gorgeous scenery with one-tenth the crowds of the South Rim. Because of its cool, high elevation, the North Rim is covered in alpine forests of spruce, fir, and aspen, giving it a feel more like the Rockies than the desert Southwest.

Colorado River (p.199)

Often referred to as the Nile of America, the Colorado flows free for 277 miles in Grand Canyon. Along the way it passes through a stunning landscape hidden from much of the outside world. Without question, a river trip through Grand Canyon is one of the most fantastic adventures on the planet.

Havasu Falls (p.285)

Part tropical paradise, part Southwestern dreamscape. Remote Havasu Canyon is home to two of the most beautiful waterfalls in North America. The only challenge is getting there.

GRAND CANYON
THE COMPLETE GUIDE

©2007 DESTINATION PRESS & ITS LICENSORS
ISBN 13: 978-0-9678904-2-5

Written & Photographed
by James Kaiser

Special thanks to Tom Pittenger, Lon Ayers, Dawn O'Sickey, Colleen Hyde, Pam Frazier, Tricia Lund, Ginger Reeve, Gray Thompson and the entire staff at Grand Canyon National Park.

As always, special thanks to my family, friends, and all the wonderful people I encountered while working on this guide.

All information in this guide has been exhaustively researched, but names, phone numbers, and other details do change. If you encounter a change or mistake while using this guide, please send an email to changes@jameskaiser.com. Your input will help make future editions of this guide even better!

Additional Photo Credits
Denver Public Library, Western History Collection, T#188: p.74
Grand Canyon National Park: p.68–#012, 69–#445, 72–#05423/08976, 73–#008/09903, 77–#11339, 78–#16237, 82–#14642b, 85–#13868, 88–#825, 89(Bill Bass)–#14718, 87–#011, 90–#02435, 92–#5281, 93–#00133, 94–#17700, 95–#09508, 96–#01573, 97–#30, 128–#16950, 129–#05423, 136–#7448, 137–#11822, 138–#16251, 139–#22596, 153–#5121A, 154–#5972, 162–#12084, 166–#12005, U.S. Wildlife stock photos: 48, 49, 50, 51, 52, 53, 55, 56, 57, 58, 59, 60, 61, 62, 63, 64, 66, 67, Bureau of Reclamation: p.100, 204, 214, 215, Library of Congress: p.81, Earth Island Institute: p.101
Peter Bohler: 14, 54, 65, 186, 188, 189, 190, 192, 194, 195, 261, 262, 264, 266, 268, 270, 278, North Wind Picture Archives: p.80, 99

Printed in China

From The Author

My FIRST INTRODUCTION to Grand Canyon was in college, driving cross country on my way to California. Starting in the east, I hit every bastion of Americana I could—Graceland, Bourbon Street, the Alamo. When I reached Grand Canyon, I parked my car and slowly walked to the rim. A life changing experience? The start of a soul-wrenching love affair that inspired my destiny as a guidebook writer? Actually, I reached into my jacket, grabbed my *instant camera* (I swear it's true!) and snapped off a few shots. After basking in the view, I climbed back into my car and headed to California.

Did I like the view? Of course. Did I realize Grand Canyon had anything else to offer? Not really. It wasn't until several years later that I realized how foolish I had been. Having stumbled into a career in photography, I was sent on a Grand Canyon river trip. It was—and still is—one of the most incredible journeys I have ever taken. For 19 days I floated down the Colorado, running rapids and hiking to dozens of spectacular sights—lush side canyons, hidden waterfalls, ancient Indian ruins. River guides, many of whom had spent *decades* rowing the Colorado, imparted their love and knowledge of the Canyon to me. By the end of the trip, I was hooked. I returned to Grand Canyon again and again, wandering the rims, hiking the trails, studying the geology, and learning as much as I could about this amazing place.

Looking back, I can't believe I ever took Grand Canyon for granted. Unfortunately, most first-time visitors continue to make the same mistake. They step out of their cars, bask in the view, and run off to their next destination. Vegas? Check. Hoover Dam? Check. Grand Canyon? Check. One of the most incredible places on *earth* and they missed it!

That's where this book comes in.

From hiking to river trips to scenic flights, Grand Canyon has it all. But it can be an incredibly overwhelming place. This book breaks it down, shows you the best of what Grand Canyon has to offer, and equips you with everything you need to make the most of your time in the park. So go for a hike, drive along the rim, or dine on a gourmet meal at a historic lodge. But whatever you do, don't peek over the rim and wonder what to do next!

INTRODUCTION

ONE MILE DEEP. Ten miles wide. One hundred sixty miles long. Covering 1.2 million acres in northern Arizona, Grand Canyon is a breathtaking act of geology. Teddy Roosevelt called it, "the one great sight every American should see." The panorama from the rim is one of the most impressive sights in the world, but Grand Canyon is so much more than just a pretty view. Hidden within its depths are fascinating creatures, geologic marvels, the ruins of an ancient civilization, and some of the best outdoor adventures in North America.

Cut by the Colorado River over the past six million years, Grand Canyon is a colossal labyrinth of towering buttes and deep side canyons. Although massive, most visitors head to one of two developed areas: the South Rim or the North Rim. The South Rim, located two hours north of Phoenix, is by far the more accessible and popular of the two. Home to six of the park's eight lodges, it's what most people think of when they think of Grand Canyon. The North Rim is located just south of the Arizona/Utah border—one of the least densely populated regions in the United States. Its remote location means fewer crowds, but with equally stunning views.

Hiking trails descend from both rims to the bottom of the Canyon. Along the way they pass though 11 layers of ancient rocks, ranging in age from 250 million to two *billion* years old—nearly half the age of the earth! At the bottom of the Canyon, near the junction of three popular trails, lies Phantom Ranch, an overnight lodge offering comfortable beds and home-cooked meals. Guided mule trips are also offered along several Grand Canyon trails; both day and overnight trips are available.

Twisting through the bottom of the Canyon is the Colorado River. Fed by Rocky Mountain snowmelt before slicing through the deserts of Utah and Arizona, the Colorado is the most impressive river in the West. Although currently plugged by dams along much of its length, the Colorado flows free in Grand Canyon, dropping 2,000 feet in 277 miles. Each year, over 20,000 people embark on river trips through Grand Canyon. In addition to 60 thrilling rapids, river trips provide access to spectacular hiking trails, stunning Indian ruins, and gorgeous waterfalls. Without question, a river trip through Grand Canyon is one of the most incredible outdoor adventures in North America.

Clearing storm

Colorado River

South Kaibab Trail

Zoroaster Temple

Bright Angel Trail

HIKING

GRAND CANYON OFFERS some of the best hiking in the Southwest. The range of scenery in the park is incredible, from cool pine forests to narrow slot canyons to everything else in between. There are trails that skirt the edge of the rim and trails that plunge thousands of feet to the Colorado River. And don't forget the Canyon's two billion years of amazing geology—arranged chronologically for your viewing pleasure.

Sound too good to be true? Not at all. But before you hit the trail there are some important things that you need to know. First, there are two types of hikes in Grand Canyon: day hikes and backcountry (overnight) hikes. Day hikes are very straightforward—just pick a hike and go. Backcountry hikes, however, require a bit more planning. Due to the large number of visitors interested in backcountry hiking, the National Park Service limits the total number of backcountry hikers allowed on each trail to reduce crowding and maintain the wilderness experience. Backcountry hikers must apply for permits, which are granted on a first-come, first-served basis.

Grand Canyon has many amazing Inner Canyon trails. But unlike most hikes on the planet, Inner Canyon trails start at the top and end at the bottom. This "mountain-in-reverse" style of hiking poses several unique challenges. For starters, a hike into the Canyon seems deceptively easy on the way down. Each year park rangers rescue hundreds of hikers who overestimate their hiking ability and become stranded near the bottom of the Canyon. In general, it takes about twice as long to hike *up* to the rim as it takes to hike *down* to the Colorado River. Another factor is temperature—the lower you go, the hotter it gets, with temperatures up to 20°F hotter at the bottom of the Canyon. Despite these challenges, hiking in Grand Canyon is a fantastic experience. Just follow the rules and tips on the following pages and your trip will be safe and enjoyable.

If hiking in Grand Canyon still seems a bit intimidating, the Grand Canyon Field Institute (GCFI) offers a variety of excellent backpacks, day hikes, and rim walks led by experienced guides. The GCFI, which works in partnership with the National Park Service, is dedicated to enhancing the understanding and enjoyment of the Grand Canyon through firsthand experience. Their highly recommended activities accommodate a wide range of ages and abilities. For more information visit www.grandcanyon.org/fieldinstitute.

DAY HIKES

There are two types of day hikes in Grand Canyon: day hikes along the rim and day hikes that descend partway down the Canyon along Inner Canyon trails. The North Rim has the most day hikes along the rim with about half a dozen popular trails. The South Rim only has one day hike along the rim: the Rim Trail, which passes by many of the South Rim's most popular viewpoints. The South Rim also has several popular Inner Canyon trails that can be followed partway down as a dayhike. If you plan on dayhiking in the Canyon, know your limits and give yourself plenty of time to return before sundown.

BACKCOUNTRY HIKES

If you're thirsting for more than a quick day hike, Grand Canyon offers a number of spectacular backcountry hikes that start at the rim and descend into the Canyon. These hikes, best tackled over multiple days, are called backcountry hikes because they follow trails that pass through terrain classified by the park as "backcountry." The park service has divided the backcountry into four management zones: Corridor, Threshold, Primitive, and Wild.

Corridor Zone trails are well-maintained and equipped with modern facilities. There are three Corridor trails in Grand Canyon: the Bright Angel Trail, South Kaibab Trail, and North Kaibab Trail. Not surprisingly, these trails are the most popular backcountry hikes in the park. Because Corridor Zone trails are heavily trafficked and provide relatively easy access to water, Backcountry Rangers strongly recommend that first-time Grand Canyon backcountry hikers stick to Corridor Zone trails.

The Threshold Zone offers trails that are officially unmaintained but generally in fair condition. There are two Threshold trails covered in this book: the Hermit Trail and the Grandview Trail.

The final two management zones, Primitive and Wild, cover extremely rugged terrain beyond the abilities of most Grand Canyon visitors. The Thunder River Trail is the only Primitive Zone trail covered in this book. Considerable Grand Canyon hiking experience is necessary in Primitive and Wild zones.

To camp in the backcountry, you must apply for a permit from the park Backcountry Office. Be aware that the backcountry is divided into "Use Areas" delineated on commercial maps. Knowing which Use Area a trail traverses is necessary when applying for a backcountry permit. Note that camping in the Corridor, Hermit, Monument, Horseshoe Mesa, and Tapeats Use Areas is limited to designated campsites or campgrounds, and camping there is limited to two nights per hike. (From Nov. 15 to Feb. 28, however, you can camp up to four nights in popular corridor campgrounds.)

BACKCOUNTRY PERMITS

Permits are required for all overnight backcountry hikes. Each year the National Park Service receives about 30,000 requests for about 13,000 available permits. Although these numbers seem intimidating, if you plan in advance a permit isn't too hard to come by. On short notice, however, a backcountry permit can be very difficult to obtain, especially in the busy summer months.

Backcountry permits are issued by the Backcountry Reservation Office. The earliest a permit can be requested is on the first day of the month, four months prior to the proposed start date. That is, if you want to apply for a permit sometime in June—June 1, June 15, June 30, etc.—the earliest you can apply is February 1. Permit requests can be submitted via mail or fax, but they are considered late if they are not received at least three weeks prior to the proposed start date. The backcountry permit request form is available on Grand Canyon's official website Permit requests are processed in the order they're received. All written requests are responded to via U.S. Mail (allow at least three weeks for processing). For detailed information on the backcountry permit process visit Grand Canyon's website or call 928-638-7875 Monday–Friday, 1 pm–5 pm.

www.nps.gov/grca/planyourvisit/backcountry-permit.htm

Mailing Address:
Backcountry Information Center
Grand Canyon National Park
PO Box 129
Grand Canyon, AZ 86023

Fax: 928-638-2125

Although most people request permits well ahead of time, cancellations sometimes make same-day permits available. You can place yourself on a waiting list for same-day permits if you arrive at the Backcountry Information Center by 8 a.m. on the day that you'd like to hike. The South Rim Backcountry Office is located to the east of Maswik Lodge, next to the railroad tracks.

PERMIT FEES

There is a non-refundable $10 fee per permit, plus $5 per person per night below the rim ($5 per group above the rim). Permit cancellations are subject to a $10 cancellation fee. Frequent hikers can purchase a one-year Frequent Hiker membership for $25 that waives the initial $10 fee for each permit. If a permit is cancelled three days or more before the start date, the $5 per person fee can be applied to a future hike.

HIKING TIPS

Don't hike to the river and back in a single day
Each year the park service rescues hundreds of day hikers stranded in the Canyon. Hiking to the river and back seems deceptively easy on the way down. By the time a weary hiker realizes how difficult the hike back up will be, it's often too late. Evacuations are time consuming and costly. (Helicopter evacuations can cost a stranded hiker upwards of $3,000 per flight.) By planning ahead and understanding the trail, you can easily avoid a needless evacuation.

Bring plenty of water
The biggest dangers on the trail are not scorpions, rattlesnakes, or mountain lions—in fact, these animals pose relatively little threat—but dehydration, heat exhaustion, and heat stroke. Rangers recommend drinking one gallon of water per day in the summer. Drink small amounts often, even if you don't feel thirsty. By the time you feel thirsty, you're already dehydrated. Some trails have access to water, but many do not. Ask about a trail's water availability before you start hiking, and filter or purify all water from springs, creeks, etc.

Use extreme caution when hiking in the summer
In the sweltering summer months, heat-related dangers—dehydration, heat exhaustion, heat stroke—become even more pronounced. Temperatures rise as you descend into the Canyon. The average temperature at the Colorado River is roughly 20°F higher than the temperature along the rim. The best way to stay safe is to avoid hiking during the middle of the day and to drink plenty of water.

Bring plenty of food
Just as important as drinking is eating. Salty snacks replace electrolytes that the body loses through sweating. If you drink water but don't replace electrolytes, you run the risk of developing hyponatremia, which can lead to seizures and sometimes death. When hiking in the Canyon, eat more than you normally do, and eat small amounts often. Every time you drink, you should also eat.

Check backcountry conditions online
The park's official website (www.nps.gov/grca) has a "Backcountry Updates and Closures" page that offers current information about backcountry conditions.

Make way for mules
Mules have the right of way on all trails. If you encounter mules, step off the trail on the uphill side and obey the directions of the mule wrangler.

Use common sense
Don't take shortcuts, don't approach wild animals, and don't engage in reckless behavior. Use common sense and know your limits.

FLASH & DEBRIS FLOODS FLOWS

FLASH FLOODS ARE one of Grand Canyon's greatest dangers. Although dry for much of the year, heavy rains pound Grand Canyon in late summer. During monsoon season—July, August, and early September—thunderstorms sweep through the region on an almost daily basis, sometimes dumping several inches of rain in a few hours. The rocky, sun-baked landscape and sparse vegetation does little to absorb the water or slow it down. Runoff from these storms is channeled into side canyons, and if the rain is heavy and the side canyon drains a large area, a flash flood can form. Racing through side canyons at speeds topping 23 feet *per second*, flash floods often push forward a wall of water several feet high. The force of this flood is so powerful that it compresses the air in front, sending pebbles and small rocks flying through the air in advance of the approaching wall of water.

Even more frightening, flash floods can form when skies are clear and sunny overhead. Storms in the region tend to be highly localized, dumping several inches of rain over a concentrated area. Land a few miles distant often remains dry. In the late summer of 1997, 12 tourists were hiking through Antelope Canyon (not far from Grand Canyon) when a thunderstorm 10 miles distant dumped an inch and a half of rain in less than an hour. The runoff from this storm gathered with astonishing speed, sending an 11-foot wall of water roaring through Antelope Canyon. The flood killed all but one of the hikers. The sole survivor had been pressed against the canyon wall, gasping for air as the flood raged past. By the time the water subsided, every stitch of clothing on his body except his boots had been ripped off by the muddy, gritty water.

Similar to flash floods—but even more destructive—are debris flows. Unlike flash floods, which are 80–90 percent water, debris flows are a deadly slurry of water, rocks, and debris—up to 60 percent solid material by volume. Roaring through side canyons at speeds up to 25 feet *per second*—three feet per second *faster* than flash floods—debris flows rip out trees and wash away boulders weighing hundreds of tons. On average, two debris flows are triggered in the Grand Canyon each year. Though few people have ever seen a debris flow, the resulting vibration shakes the ground for miles.

MULE TRIPS

FOR OVER A century, mule trips have been one of Grand Canyon's most popular activities. Everyone from Teddy Roosevelt to The Brady Bunch has descended the Canyon on mule, and while hardcore hikers would never dream of passing up a chance to hike into the Canyon, for many people mules are the only way to go. These sure-footed animals are fun, convenient, and offer a genuine taste of the Old West. (And did I mention they do most of the hard work for you?)

Although less demanding than hiking, mule riding is still a physical activity. Riders must sit up straight on a moving animal for extended periods of time, which requires more endurance than you might think. And then there's the fear factor. Mules are incredibly safe animals, but they often walk terrifyingly close to the edge of the trail. Sometimes it seems like they're doing this intentionally just to taunt you with their amazing sense of balance. In other words, mule riding is not for the faint of heart. But despite a few mild challenges, most people have no problems riding mules, and many consider the experience to be great fun.

The South Rim offers both day and overnight mule trips. Day trips head down the Bright Angel Trail to Plateau Point, arriving back in Grand Canyon Village by mid-afternoon. Overnight trips follow the Bright Angel Trail to the bottom of the Canyon, where riders spend the night at Phantom Ranch, a small lodge offering beds and home-cooked meals. Riders return the next morning via the South Kaibab Trail. Two-night trips are also available from mid-November through March. Reservations for South Rim mule trips are accepted up to a year in advance and are highly recommended for the busy summer months. The North Rim only offers day trips, including trips along the rim and trips that descend partway down the North Kaibab Trail.

No experience is necessary for a mule trip, but riders must be at least 4 feet 7 inches tall (1.38 m), weigh less than 200 pounds (91 kg), and speak fluent English so the mule can understand commands.

South Rim Mule Trips: p.117
North Rim Mule Trips: p.257

Colorado River Trips

A RIVER TRIP through Grand Canyon is one of the most incredible outdoor adventures in North America. From fighting off frothing rapids to hiking up dramatic side canyons, the memories you'll gain on a Grand Canyon river trip will last a lifetime.

Over a dozen commercial outfitters are licensed to offer guided river trips through Grand Canyon. Trips range in length from one day to nineteen days, and they generally cost between $200 and $300 per person per day. The best trips are the multi-day adventures run between Lees Ferry (river mile 0) and Diamond Creek (river mile 226). One- to three-day "sampler" trips run at either end of the Canyon don't even come close to the scenery found in the heart of the park. Some companies also offer trips geared to specific interests such as hiking, photography or natural history. But due to the immense popularity of all river trips and the limited number of passengers the national park service allows on the river each year, many trips are booked up to a year in advance.

Commercial outfitters run trips with both motorized and non-motorized boats. Motorized boats speed through the Canyon, allowing you to visit more sights in less time. While some people find this convenient, others dislike the whirlwind pace. Non-motorized boats come in two varieties: inflatable rafts and dories. Inflatable rafts cushion the impact of the rapids, resulting in a smoother ride. Rigid dories, piloted by skilled boatmen, offer a more tumultuous ride where flipping is a distinct possibility. But flipping is generally rare, and for many thrill seekers elegant dory boats are the only way to go.

River-running season in Grand Canyon generally lasts from mid-April through early November. Summer is the most popular season, but it's also the worst time to go due to heavy crowds and scorching temperatures. The best time for a river trip is in the spring or the fall, when temperatures are mild and the river is much less crowded. Private, noncommercial river trips are also allowed, but the waiting list for a permit is often several years.

For more on running the Colorado River through Grand Canyon, see the Colorado River chapter (p.199).

RIVER OUTFITTERS

Arizona Raft Adventures
(800-786-7238 www.azraft.com)

Arizona River Runners
(800-477-7238, www.raftaz.com)

Canyon Explorations/Expeditions
(800-654-0723, www.canyonexplorations.com)

Canyoneers
(800-525-0924, www.canyoneers.com)

Colorado River and Trail Expeditions
(800-253-7328, www.crateinc.com)

Diamond River Adventures
(800-343-3121, www.diamondriver.com)

Grand Canyon Expeditions Company
(800-544-2691, www.gcex.com)

Hatch River Expeditions
(800-856-8966, www.hatchriverexpeditions.com)

Moki Mac River Expeditions
(800-284-7280, www.mokimac.com)

O.A.R.S./Grand Canyon Dories
(800-346-6277, www.oars.com)

Outdoors Unlimited
(800-637-7238, www.outdoorsunlimited.com)

Tour West
(800-453-9107, www.twriver.com)

Western River Expeditions
(866-904-1160, www.westernriver.com)

Wilderness River Adventures
(800-992-8022, www.riveradventures.com)

CHOOSE YOUR WEAPON

OAR-POWERED RAFT

Oar-powered rafts offer a great mix of safety and excitement. Their flexibility allows them to bounce off obstacles and absorb much of a rapid's energy, resulting in a smoother ride. Tipping is rarely a problem, but expect to get wet. Some outfitters allow passengers to help paddle rafts.

DORY BOAT

These elegant boats, paddled only by guides, require the most skill to maneuver. Because they're made of rigid wood or fiberglass, dories ride like a roller coaster through the rapids (and occasionally flip over). But they provide the most rugged and exciting ride Grand Canyon has to offer.

MOTORIZED J-RIG

J-Rigs are the biggest, most stable craft on the Colorado. Because they accommodate up to 20 people, they transport the majority of commercial passengers in Grand Canyon. J-Rigs speed through the Canyon faster than non-motorized boats, which can be a good or a bad thing, depending on your preference.

SCENIC FLIGHTS

NO MATTER HOW much time you've spent peering over the rim of Grand Canyon, nothing can prepare you for the perspective you'll gain from the air. Viewed from above, the colossal maze of temples and buttes stretches all the way to the horizon, revealing some of the Canyon's most remote scenery.

More than 100,000 scenic flights soar over Grand Canyon each year. Grand Canyon Airport in Tusayan—the small town located a few miles south of the South Rim's main entrance—offers both airplane and helicopter flights. The main difference between an airplane flight and a helicopter flight is the speed and elevation at which they fly. Air-safety regulations require airplanes to fly about 1,000 feet higher than helicopters. Most people prefer helicopter flights, which provide a slower ride and a closer view, but airplane flights allow you to cover more ground in less time—and for less money. Depending on the route, helicopter flights last 25–45 minutes, while airplane flights last 45–90 minutes. Airplane flights generally cost $120–$300; helicopter flights generally cost $175–$235. (Discounts for children are often available for both.)

To reduce noise pollution, strict regulations limit which parts of the park scenic flights can explore. All told, over 75 percent of the park is off limits, including the air space above popular viewpoints on the North and South Rims and the "corridor zone" between them. Furthermore, no aircraft are allowed below the rim within the boundaries of the park. Despite these restrictions, scenic flights still reveal some of the Canyon's most beautiful scenery, most of which would remain hidden unless viewed from the air.

HELICOPTER FLIGHTS

Grand Canyon Helicopters (800-541-4537, www.grandcanyonhelicoptersaz.com)
Maverick Helicopters (866-689-8687, www.maverickhelicopter.com)
Papillon (800-528-2418, www.papillon.com)

AIRPLANE FLIGHTS

Air Grand Canyon (800-247-4726, www.airgrandcanyon.com)
Grand Canyon Airlines (866-235-9422, www.grandcanyonairlines.com)

National Canyon

GEOLOGY

GRAND CANYON IS a geological wonderland. There are few locations on the planet with so many eye-popping rock formations on display in a single place. It's safe to say that, had they been located elsewhere, many of these individual rock formations would be world-famous landmarks on their own. But within the depths of the Canyon they occur by the dozen. Rainbow-splashed mesas, temples, and buttes cascade down from the rim, extending for miles in either direction. Visually, there is so much to see—so many colors, textures, and shadows—that your sense of perspective melts away. The scope of the scenery is dizzying, which is what makes staring out into Grand Canyon so much fun.

Even if you know nothing about geology, Grand Canyon is still an impressive sight. But take the time to learn about the forces that created it, and you'll look upon the Canyon with a fresh set of eyes. Suddenly, what was once amazing will become astounding. What once took your breath away will make your head spin.

On a human timescale, Grand Canyon seems ancient, peaceful, and serene. On a geologic timescale, however, it is young, violent, and exciting. Geologists were shocked to discover that Grand Canyon was created in less than six million years. When you consider that the earth is over four *billion* years old, six million years seems like the blink of an eye. It's as if northern Arizona suddenly just cracked open and—*bam!*—there was Grand Canyon.

In reality, northern Arizona was sliced open by the Colorado River. After tumbling down from the Rockies, the Colorado twists and turns through the desert Southwest, picking up an enormous amount of sediment along the way. This sediment—a mixture of gravel, silt and clay eroded from the region's soft rocks—scrapes along the bottom of the river like sandpaper, cutting downward at a rate of about 6.5 inches every 1,000 years. Over the past six million years, the Colorado has sliced through northern Arizona like a knife through a wedding cake. In the process it has exposed dozens of layers of progressively older rocks, giving Grand Canyon one of its most defining characteristics: it is one of the few places in the world where you can view almost two billion years of earth history just by glancing up and down.

ANCIENT ROCKS

MOST ROCKS IN Grand Canyon are sedimentary rocks, which form when sediments such as sand, silt, or mud gather in thick layers that, over time, are compressed into rock. Grand Canyon's sedimentary rock layers accumulated over millions of years on the prehistoric surface of northern Arizona, which has been home to giant sand dunes, muddy river deltas, and shallow tropical seas over the past 500 million years. These environments formed as ancient continents drifted across the globe and ancient oceans advanced and retreated over those continents. Eventually, eroded sediments from each of these environments formed distinct layers of sedimentary rocks. Sand dunes were cemented into sandstone, mud was compressed into shale, and the discarded shells of marine animals were cemented together into limestone.

Because Grand Canyon's rocks were laid down chronologically, one on top of another, they reflect a geological relationship known as *superposition*. Simply put, superposition means that the rocks above are younger than the rocks below. Move your eyes from the rim to the river and you are essentially staring back into time. At the bottom of the Canyon we find the region's oldest exposed rocks: Vishnu Schist and Zoroaster Granite. These rocks, referred to as the Precambrian Rocks of the Inner Gorge, are the only common rocks in Grand Canyon that are not sedimentary. Vishnu Schist is a metamorphic rock that formed roughly 1.7 billion years ago when intense heat and pressure transformed previously formed shale into schist. About 200 million years later, magma shot up into cracks in the schist and cooled into beautiful veins of pink Zoroaster Granite.

It wasn't until about 550 million years ago that the Tapeats Sandstone, the oldest major sedimentary rock in Grand Canyon, started to form. What happened in the one billion years between the formation of the Vishnu Schist and the Tapeats Sandstone is a bit of a mystery. During that time, up to 12,000 feet of additional rocks formed on top of the Vishnu Schist. But by 570 million years ago those additional rocks had eroded away, leaving an enormous gap in the geologic record. Geologists refer to such a gap as an unconformity. In Grand Canyon, the gap between the Vishnu Schist and the Tapeats Sandstone is known as the Great Unconformity—a name given by the early explorer John Wesley Powell. After the formation of the Tapeats Sandstone, additional sedimentary rock layers continued to accumulate. The youngest sedimentary rock in Grand Canyon is the 260 million year-old Kaibab Limestone, familiar to anyone who has walked along the South Rim.

Another rock formation found in Grand Canyon is the Grand Canyon Supergroup. These rocks started out as sedimentary rocks around one billion years ago, but they were later metamorphosed by heat and pressure. Today rocks from the Grand Canyon Supergroup are only visible from a handful of locations in Grand Canyon, such as Lipan Point on the South Rim.

The thought grew in my mind that the canyons of this region would be a Book of Revelations in the rock-leaved Bible of geology. The thought fructified and I determined to read the book.

—John Wesley Powell

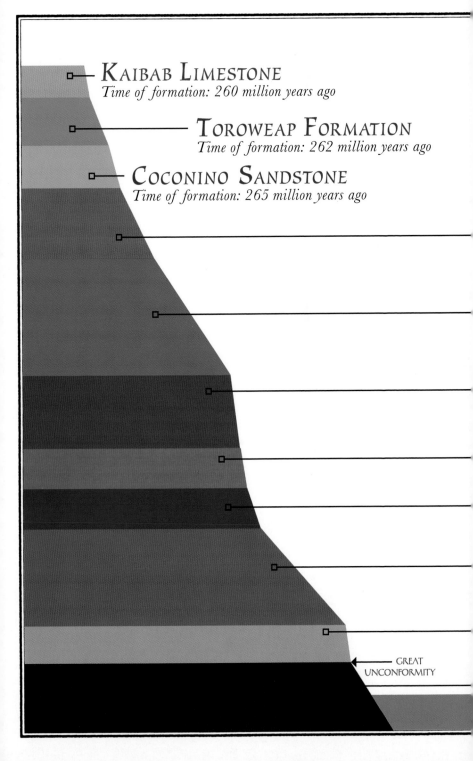

KAIBAB LIMESTONE
Time of formation: 260 million years ago

TOROWEAP FORMATION
Time of formation: 262 million years ago

COCONINO SANDSTONE
Time of formation: 265 million years ago

GREAT
UNCONFORMITY

GRAND CANYON ROCK LAYERS

—— HERMIT SHALE
Time of formation: 270 million years ago

—————————— SUPAI GROUP
Time of formation: 270-320 million years ago

—— REDWALL LIMESTONE
Time of formation: 340 million years ago

—————————— TEMPLE BUTTE LIMESTONE
Time of formation: 370 million years ago

— MUAV LIMESTONE
Time of formation: 530 million years ago

—————————— BRIGHT ANGEL SHALE
Time of formation: 540 million years ago

— TAPEATS SANDSTONE
Time of formation: 550 million years ago

—————————— VISHNU SCHIST
Time of formation: 1.7–1.5 billion years ago

THE COLORADO PLATEAU

THE SEDIMENTS THAT formed the sedimentary rocks in Grand Canyon generally accumulated at or near sea level. So how did they end up thousands of feet above sea level? The answer has to do with Grand Canyon's location on the southwestern edge of a huge area known as the Colorado Plateau. This area, filled with some of the most stunning natural features in America, encompasses much of the Four Corners region (Arizona, Utah, Colorado and New Mexico).

Starting around 60 million years ago, forces within the earth began pushing up the Colorado Plateau. By about five million years ago, it had risen over a vertical mile. The higher elevation led to increased precipitation, which led to increased erosion that stripped away many of the region's rocks. During this time several thousand feet of overlying rocks were removed above the Kaibab Limestone (the top-most rock layer in Grand Canyon today).

As erosion chipped away at the Four Corners region, it sculpted one of the most dramatic landscapes in the world. But aside from their physical beauty, the sedimentary rocks of the Colorado Plateau are notable because they are so exquisitely preserved. This is due to the relative stability (geologically speaking) of the Colorado Plateau. As continents have drifted across the globe over the past 600 million years, smashing into one another and deforming the crust of the earth, the Colorado Plateau has been sheltered from much of the action. As a result, its sedimentary layers remain relatively intact. By contrast, the rock layers in the geologically active regions surrounding the Colorado Plateau, such as the Great Basin and Rocky Mountains, have been severely deformed.

Some geologists believe the Colorado Plateau has resisted deformation so successfully because the earth's crust is relatively thick in the Four Corners region. In places, the crust beneath the Colorado Plateau is up to 25 miles thick. The crust of the Great Basin Desert, by comparison, is only 16 miles thick. So rather than buckle and break as it was pushed upward, the Colorado Plateau has remained relatively unaltered as a single tectonic block.

The uplift of the Colorado Plateau continues today. By some estimates, it has risen as much as 1,000 feet over the past one million years. During this time,

there have been some notable geologic hiccups along its boundaries. In western Grand Canyon, which lies near the boundary of the Colorado Plateau and the Great Basin, the earth's crust is thinner and more broken. As a result, hundreds of volcanoes have erupted near western Grand Canyon over the past two million years. At least 150 eruptions have sent lava pouring over the rim of the Canyon and tumbling down to the Colorado River. When the lava cooled, it often formed massive dams that backed up the river for miles. The largest dam, called Prospect Dam, was over 2,300 feet high. It created a massive reservoir that took 22 years to fill and stretched all the way to Moab, Utah. But in as little as 20,000 years, the gritty Colorado completely eroded Prospect Dam.

THE COLORADO RIVER

THE COLORADO RIVER, more than anything, is responsible for the creation of Grand Canyon. But that's only part of the story. The specifics are considerably more complex. Early geologists, starting with John Wesley Powell, assumed that the modern river has always flowed along its present course. The way they saw it, the river cut down into northern Arizona as the Colorado Plateau rose up around it.

Then, in the 1930s and '40s, geologists came to the startling conclusion that the Colorado has not always followed its present course. Although the ancestral Colorado did flow into northern Arizona, passing through the region that would one day become eastern Grand Canyon, it avoided western Grand Canyon entirely. Rather than flow west through Arizona, it flowed *north* into Utah!

This led to a frustrating dilemma: if the early Colorado avoided western Grand Canyon entirely, how did western Grand Canyon form? That question has yet to be answered definitively. Much of the evidence has long since eroded away, so facts are hard to come by. But geologists have been able to piece together a general theory. Back when the ancestral Colorado flowed north into Utah, a second "lower" Colorado River originated somewhere to the west of Grand Canyon. Over time, the headwaters of the lower Colorado eroded east until they reached the western edge of the Colorado Plateau. As they continued to carve away at the landscape, the headwaters came closer and closer to the upper Colorado. Then, around five million years ago, a critical divide was breached between the two rivers. The lower Colorado captured the upper Colorado, and the upper Colorado started flowing west. At that moment, the modern Colorado River was born.

For the next five million years, the modern Colorado bore down into the landscape as the Colorado Plateau rose up around it—pretty much the way early geologists envisioned it. But the river's rate of downward cutting has not been constant. Its cutting power varied considerably depending on which rocks the river cut through. Soft sedimentary rocks (such as shale) were cut through quickly, while harder sedimentary rocks (such as limestone) took much longer.

At any rate, the Colorado cut through all of the sedimentary rocks in a remarkably short period of time. By about 3.8 million years ago, Grand Canyon was within 500 feet of its current depth. The river was now grinding through Vishnu Schist—the hardest rock in the Canyon—and its rate of downward cutting slowed significantly. At the same time, another characteristic of the river started to change. As the Colorado ground down the steep obstacles that once choked the river, its grade began to level out. Because rivers with gentle grades are much less erosive than rivers with steep grades, the Colorado's rate of downward cutting was further reduced. Over the past one million years, the river has cut down less than 50 feet.

This shocking fact reveals a tremendous amount about the creation of Grand Canyon. While the Colorado sliced into northern Arizona like a band saw between three and five million years ago, it has done relatively little since then. Contrary to popular belief, erosion in Grand Canyon does not occur at a steady rate. Rather, it happens in brief spurts when powerful forces pound away at the landscape. Periods of intense erosion almost always correspond to periods when massive obstacles—lava dams, the uplift of the Colorado Plateau—block an easy path for the river. The Colorado doesn't just find the path of least resistance, it creates it, which gives one pause when considering the ultimate fate of the man-made obstacles (dams) that hold back the river today.

THE CANYON GROWS

ALTHOUGH THE COLORADO River is remarkably good at cutting down, it barely makes a dent horizontally. In fact, the river often *adds* inches to the riverbank by depositing sediment. Yet in places Grand Canyon is over 10 miles wide. What's going on here?

Although the Colorado carved out a remarkably deep channel, the width of Grand Canyon is mostly due to runoff from the rim. In both cases the mechanics are similar—gritty water grinds down the region's soft rocks, breaking them down into sediment that's flushed out of the Canyon. But while most of the water in the Colorado River comes from the Rocky Mountains, runoff from the rim falls on northern Arizona in the form of rain and snow. In effect, the Colorado's deep channel serves as a giant template, funneling much of the surrounding runoff into the Canyon.

But the rate of erosion along Grand Canyon's walls has not been constant. The walls of the North Rim have eroded up to 10 times faster than the walls of the South Rim. This has nothing to do with the rocks that are being eroded—the two rims share the same rocks—but rather the amount of precipitation that tumbles down from each rim. Both sides of the Grand Canyon are tilted slightly to the south. As a result, precipitation that falls on the North Rim runs *into* the Canyon, while precipitation that falls on the South Rim runs *away* from the Canyon. Because the North Rim receives much more runoff, its walls have eroded at a significantly faster rate—a fact readily apparent to anyone who has visited both sides of the Canyon. Viewed from the South Rim, the walls of the North Rim gradually recede into the distance. But viewed from the North Rim, the walls of the South Rim are incredibly steep.

Despite strikingly different slopes, both rims cascade down to the Colorado River in a series of craggy temples and buttes. This is also due to variable rates of erosion. Just as the Colorado has cut down through the Canyon's rocks at different rates, the same rocks have eroded horizontally at different rates as well. Soft rocks erode easily to form gentle slopes, while hard rocks resist erosion to form steep cliffs. This stairstep formation of rock layers is one of the defining characteristics of Grand Canyon. To frequent hikers, the familiar slopes and cliffs provide a constant reminder of where one is in the Canyon.

Grand Canyon is also famous for its deep side canyons, which often form along faults where the land has lifted or subsided, creating a narrow channel where runoff accumulates. Over thousands of years, the runoff carves out a deep side canyon. The creation of a side canyon is a self-reinforcing process. The larger the side canyon becomes, the more runoff it collects; the more runoff it collects, the larger the side canyon becomes.

Although flowing water causes most erosion in Grand Canyon, other forces are also at work. *Frost wedging* occurs when water freezes and expands in the cracks of rocks, producing massive pressures—up to 20,000 pounds per square inch—that split rocks apart. In some cases, frost wedging triggers rockfalls that send massive chunks of the Canyon tumbling down to the river.

Rockfalls also occur when soft rocks erode beneath hard rocks, creating a pronounced overhang that ultimately collapses under its own weight. This process is referred to as slab failure. In Grand Canyon, with its many alternate layers of hard and soft rocks, slab failure is quite common. It's the reason why many of the Canyon's hard rock layers erode to form steep cliffs.

Ultimately, the creation of Grand Canyon was due to many factors. Rock formation, erosion, tectonic forces—all conspired to create the stunning landscape now on display. Millions of years from now, those same forces will have rendered Grand Canyon unrecognizable. So consider yourself lucky. You're alive for that brief moment (geologically speaking) when you can explore one of earth's most amazing natural features.

ECOLOGY

MORE SUBTLE THAN Grand Canyon's geology, but equally fascinating, is the park's ecology. First-time visitors often assume the Canyon is barren and lifeless. In fact, this is anything but the case. Over 6,000 feet of sudden elevation change creates a stunning range of life zones, all lying remarkably close to one another. Nowhere is this more apparent than the North Kaibab Trail, which starts in the cool boreal forest of the North Rim and ends up in the scorching desert at the bottom of the Canyon. In a matter of hours, hikers pass spruce trees and cacti, the equivalent of traveling from Canada to Mexico in a single day.

The wide range of biodiversity in Grand Canyon is due, more than anything else, to temperature and precipitation, both of which are affected by elevation. Generally speaking, temperatures rise and aridity increases as you descend into the Canyon. From the rim to the river, the contrast between environments is often extreme. At the sweltering bottom of western Grand Canyon, an average of six inches of rain falls a year, and only rugged desert plants such as cacti and yucca can survive. The cool, high plateaus of the North Rim, however, generally receive over 30 inches of precipitation a year, supporting dense forests of spruce, fir, and aspen.

The Canyon's wide range of climates also affects the distribution of animals. Cold-blooded reptiles that thrive in the warm Inner Canyon are much less common on the rim, and rim dwellers that require a steady source of water fare poorly throughout much of the Inner Canyon. Animals are also affected by the distribution of plants. Because plants form the foundation of a healthy food chain, they play a vital role in determining which animals can live where.

Plants are also dependent on animals. Consider the relationship between the pinyon pine and the pinyon jay, a pale blue bird found throughout the Colorado Plateau. Pinyon pines produce large seeds too heavy to be dispersed by the wind. But the seeds are a staple of the pinyon jay's diet. After gathering the nuts, the bird buries them for later use, but some seeds are inevitably forgotten. Those forgotten seeds often grow into new trees. Thus, pinyon pines provide the jays with an important source of food, and the pinyon jays ensure a healthy population of pinyon pines.

When viewed as a whole, the plants and animals of a particular area form unique, interdependent communities called "biotic communities." From tropical rainforests to Arctic tundra, biotic communities are found in every environment in the world. In Grand Canyon, there are six major biotic communities: boreal forests, ponderosa forests, pinyon-juniper woodland, desert scrub, and the lush riparian habitat along the banks of the Colorado River. With the exception of the riparian habitat, these biotic communities generally form horizontal bands across Grand Canyon.

Because elevation has such a profound affect on climate, it seems reasonable to assume that biotic communities could be determined based on elevation. Although elevation provides a rough approximation of where certain biotic communities might occur, many local environmental factors also come into play. Furthermore, many plants and animals live in more than one biotic community. In Grand Canyon, where a large number of biotic communities are packed tightly together, their boundaries become even more blurred.

Biotic communities are also affected by microclimates—small pockets of temperature and moisture that vary dramatically from their immediate surroundings. Microclimates are caused by a variety of environmental factors including local topography, proximity to water, and exposure to sunlight. South-facing slopes, for example, receive much more sunlight than north-facing slopes, making them significantly warmer and drier, even at higher elevations. This explains why desert plants such as yucca are found at high elevations on the south-facing North Rim, while shady pockets along the South Rim support small populations of Douglas-fir, a tree that generally avoids the South Rim's warmer, drier climate.

C. HART MERRIAM

The concept of biotic communities, "life zones" where specific groups of plants and animals interact, was first developed at Grand Canyon by the biologist C. Hart Merriam. In 1889 Merriam, then director of the U.S. Biological Survey, led an expedition to Grand Canyon to study the region's plants and animals. As he descended into the Canyon, he noticed distinct communities of plants and animals living together. He called these communities "life zones," and theorized that their location was due to the different temperature zones they occupied. Additional research would show that life zones are dependant on much more than temperature alone, Merriam's Grand Canyon expedition was the first time plants and animals were studied living together in a quantifiable way. His groundbreaking work helped pave the way for the modern study of ecology.

GRAND CANYON WEATHER

Because Grand Canyon is located in the arid Southwest, it receives much less precipitation than most parts of the country. Although precipitation is minimal, it arrives in a fairly predictable pattern, falling in the winter and summer in a nearly 50/50 split.

In the summer prevailing winds arrive from the south, carrying moisture from the Gulf of California. As moist air passes over Arizona, it's lifted up and over the highlands just south of Grand Canyon, arriving at the Canyon cool and condensed. In the morning, when the sun heats the Inner Canyon, hot air rises up and collides with the cool, moist air above. This sudden collision creates short-lived afternoon thunderstorms. In July, August and early September ("monsoon season"), these storms pound Grand Canyon on an almost daily basis.

SUMMER

WINTER

In the winter, prevailing winds arrive from the west or northwest, bringing moist air from the Pacific. Although the vast majority of this moisture is wrung out by the Sierra Nevada Mountains, some moisture does find its way into northern Arizona. Winter storms in Grand Canyon are much less intense than summer storms, but they often linger for days.

In the spring and fall Grand Canyon becomes extremely arid, resulting in dramatic temperature swings. Dry air allows up to 90 percent of solar radiation to reach the ground during the day. At night, however, the situation is reversed; 90 percent of the Canyon's accumulated heat radiates back into the atmosphere through clear, dry skies. In humid areas, by contrast, only 40 percent of solar radiation reaches the ground during the day, but that heat is often reflected back by an insulating cloud cover at night.

ICE AGE
in Grand Canyon

Twenty thousand years ago, near the peak of the last Ice Age, Grand Canyon was a markedly different place. Although the landscape was nearly identical, the distribution of plants and animals would have been unrecognizable to modern eyes. In the depths of the Ice Age, a cool, wet climate descended over the Southwest, forcing many plants and animals to retreat to lower, warmer elevations. Juniper trees, which currently grow on the South Rim, grew along the banks of the Colorado River, and Douglas-fir, a tree currently found only in the park's highest elevations, grew on the Tonto Platform 3,000 feet below the rim.

Many strange and wonderful creatures roamed the region during this time, including camels, horses and Merriam's teratorn, a bird with a wingspan more than 12 feet across. Grand Canyon was also home to the Shasta ground sloth, a massive lumbering animal that stood seven feet tall and weighed up to 400 pounds. But around 10,000 years ago many of these large prehistoric animals went extinct, most likely due to overhunting by early human settlers.

As the glaciers that covered much of North America retreated between 15,000 and 10,000 years ago, the Ice Age drew to a close. In the Southwest temperatures rose, the climate dried out, and plants and animals living in the Inner Canyon began a slow migration towards the rim. The remarkable flexibility of Grand Canyon's plants and animals—retreating to the Canyon's depths when temperatures dropped, climbing back to the rim when they warmed—is a powerful reminder that the park's seemingly fixed life zones

Air currents also affect microclimates. During the day, as the sun beats down on the region, hot air rises up the Canyon walls. Then, at night, cool air flows down from the rims. These invisible rivers of air, flowing up and down the Canyon's walls, allow a wide range of plants to survive in unlikely places in Grand Canyon.

Although life zone boundaries are often blurred by Grand Canyon's dramatic topography, the Canyon also acts as a formidable barrier to plant and animal movement. Consider the Abert squirrel, a small grayish squirrel that is entirely dependent on ponderosa pines as a source of food. During the last Ice Age, when the climate was much cooler and wetter, ponderosa forests stretched across much of northern Arizona, including the Inner Canyon. For thousands of years Abert squirrels roamed throughout the ponderosa forests in the Inner Canyon, but when temperatures started to rise around 10,000 years ago, the ponderosa pines retreated to higher elevations. Trees growing in the depths of the Canyon moved up to the rims, and with them came the Abert squirrels. Some squirrels retreated to the South Rim; others retreated to the North Rim, creating two distinct Abert squirrel populations on either side of the Canyon. Over time, the squirrels living on the North Rim developed unique physical characteristics (most notably a striking white tail) that have led scientists to classify them as an entirely separate subspecies called the Kaibab squirrel.

Dramatic fluctuations in climate have influenced the Canyon's plants and animals over the past several thousand years, but recently humans have also impacted Grand Canyon's ecology. When miners abandoned their search for Grand Canyon riches in the late 1800s, they often left their pack animals behind. Burros, originally from the deserts of Africa, were rugged enough to survive on their own, and soon they were breeding and multiplying. By the 1970s, there were as many as 350 feral burros living in Grand Canyon. Conservation groups grew concerned that the burros were competing with the Canyon's already-threatened population of bighorn sheep for scarce resources. In the late 1970s, the burros were rounded up one by one and transported out of the Canyon. Many feral burro populations remain throughout the Southwest, however, and in recent years there have been scattered reports of new feral burro populations in western Grand Canyon.

The interaction between plants, animals, and landscapes is incredibly complex in any environment. But in Grand Canyon, one of the most dynamic environments in the world, this complexity is elevated further. At times, it can be overwhelming. Even seasoned naturalists sometimes find themselves struggling to comprehend the sophisticated ecology of the park. But Grand Canyon also presents a tremendous opportunity for study and exploration. You could easily spend a lifetime learning about Grand Canyon's ecology, which is what keeps many people coming back year after year.

BALD EAGLE

Haliaeetus leucocephalus

Bald Eagles range over much of North America, including Alaska and Mexico. Although bald eagles range over a vast territory, most return to nest within 100 miles of where they were raised. Nests are reused year after year and are added to annually (some can reach up to 10 feet across and weigh up to 2,000 pounds). Bald eagles do not develop their distinctive white head until their fourth or fifth year. The "bald" in "bald eagle" is derived from an old English word meaning white. The bald eagle's scientific name, *Haliaeetus leucocephalus*, means "white-headed sea eagle." At one time there may have been as many as 75,000 bald eagles in the lower 48 states, but by the early 1960s there were fewer than 900. Hunting and habitat loss had eliminated bald eagles throughout much of their natural range. In 1967 bald eagles were placed on the federal Endangered Species List. Since then, they have made a remarkable comeback. There are now roughly 30,000 bald eagles in the lower 48 states and an additional 40,000 in Alaska.

U.S. RANGE

Found throughout Grand Canyon

INFO

WINGSPAN: 8 feet

LENGTH: 40 inches

WEIGHT: 14 pounds

LIFESPAN: 30 years

BIGHORN SHEEP

Ovis canadensis

Bighorn sheep are among the most impressive animals in Grand Canyon. Well-adapted to steep terrain, they hop along narrow ledges and jump down 20-foot inclines with grace. The ram's legendary horns take up to a decade to grow, curving up and over the ears in a C-shaped curl. A large pair of horns can weigh up to 30 pounds and reach 30 inches in length. Horns grow longer each year, but if they ever start to block peripheral vision they are broomed (deliberately rubbed down on rocks). During mating season in the fall, competing rams charge each other head on at speeds topping 20 miles per hour. When the rams collide, their horns smash together and produce a loud cracking sound that can sometimes be heard for miles. Thickened skulls allow rams to withstand repeated collisions, and rams with the biggest horns generally do the most mating. Over the past century, hunting and diseases from domestic sheep have taken a significant toll on bighorn populations in Grand Canyon.

U.S. RANGE

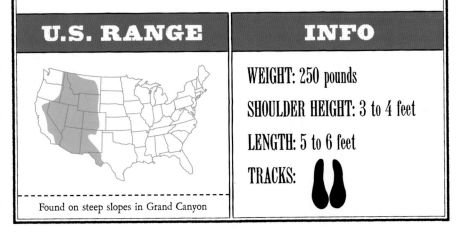

Found on steep slopes in Grand Canyon

INFO

WEIGHT: 250 pounds

SHOULDER HEIGHT: 3 to 4 feet

LENGTH: 5 to 6 feet

TRACKS:

BOBCAT

Lynx rufus

Although bobcats are North America's most common wildcat, they are elusive animals that are rarely seen or heard. They generally rest during the day, then wander for miles at night. The name "bobcat" comes from the cat's stubby bobbed tail. Bobcats are only slightly larger than house cats, and they share many of the same personality traits: hissing, purring, and sometimes using trees as scratching posts. The bobcat is closely related to the lynx, which is larger and found in colder environments. Bobcats prey on a wide range of animals including deer, rabbits, squirrels, small birds, and snakes, but rarely do they chase their prey. Bobcats seek out a hiding spot and lie patiently in wait, pouncing when a victim approaches. Bobcats are extremely solitary animals. Males and females come together only for mating. Females usually have litters of two or three kittens, although they can have as many as seven. Recent evidence indicates that bobcat populations are stable and may be increasing in places.

U.S. RANGE

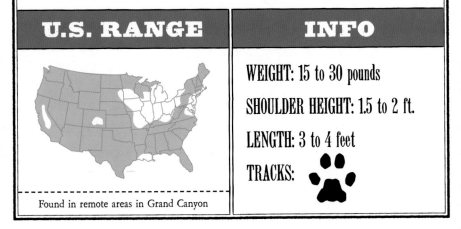

Found in remote areas in Grand Canyon

INFO

WEIGHT: 15 to 30 pounds

SHOULDER HEIGHT: 1.5 to 2 ft.

LENGTH: 3 to 4 feet

TRACKS:

CALIFORNIA CONDOR

Gymnogyps californianus

California condors are the largest, rarest birds in North America. They can be spotted soaring in the thermals above Grand Canyon, reaching speeds up to 50 mph and traveling over 100 miles per day. Although easily confused with turkey vultures, California condors have much larger wingspans and triangular white coloring on the underside of their wings. The condor's historic range once extended from Canada to Mexico, but by 1982 the worldwide California condor population had plummeted to 22 birds. Habitat loss, shootings, and animal carcasses filled with poisonous lead-shot decimated condor populations. In 1987, with the species at the brink of extinction, the last remaining birds were captured and bred in captivity. In the 1990s condors were reintroduced to central California and Grand Canyon. Although captive-bred condors have done well in the Canyon, they have yet to successfully reproduce in the wild. Condors do not reach sexual maturity until six years of age, and an adult pair typically raises only one chick every other year. But there are encouraging signs. Since 2003 a handful of condor chicks have hatched and fledged in Grand Canyon.

U.S. RANGE

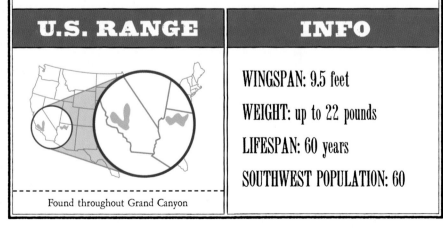

Found throughout Grand Canyon

INFO

WINGSPAN: 9.5 feet

WEIGHT: up to 22 pounds

LIFESPAN: 60 years

SOUTHWEST POPULATION: 60

ELK

Cervus elaphus

Elk are the largest member of the deer family on the Colorado Plateau. They are distinguished from mule deer by their massive size and dark brown coloration above the neck. Shawnee Indians call elk *wapiti*, "White Rump," but a male elk's most distinguishing characteristic are its massive antlers. Antlers, which are only found on bulls, can grow several feet across and weigh up to 50 pounds. They are shed each year in the spring, and over the next three to four months new antlers grow back at the rate of about half an inch a day. During rutting season in the fall, bulls emit a bugle-like sound as a sign of dominance and a challenge to other bulls. The bugle starts off as a bellow and changes to a shrill scream that can often be heard for miles. Dominance between bulls is determined in rutting contests where elk clash antlers with one another. The most dominant bulls have been known to assemble harems of up to 60 females. Elk can be very dangerous during rutting season and should never be approached.

U.S. RANGE

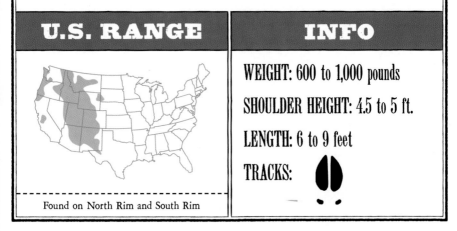

Found on North Rim and South Rim

INFO

WEIGHT: 600 to 1,000 pounds

SHOULDER HEIGHT: 4.5 to 5 ft.

LENGTH: 6 to 9 feet

TRACKS:

MOUNTAIN LION

Felis concolor

Mountain lions (also known as pumas or cougars) range from Canada to Argentina—the most extensive range of any North American mammal. At one time they inhabited all 48 lower states, but in the late 1800s and early 1900s mountain lions in the United States were hunted to the brink of extinction. Following strict hunting regulations, they have made a steady comeback in some wilderness areas, especially the Four Corners region. Mountain lions are the largest wildcats in North America. They are quick, efficient killers that can travel up to 25 miles a day in search of prey. A mountain lion will generally stalk animals within 30 feet before attacking. When they pounce they can leap up to 20 feet in a single bound, killing their victims with a lethal bite that severs the spinal cord. Mountain lions feed primarily on deer, killing up to one a week, but they also feed on elk, coyotes, and bighorn sheep. Although there has never been a mountain lion attack in Grand Canyon National Park, they have been known to attack humans elsewhere. Use extreme caution if you do encounter one.

U.S. RANGE

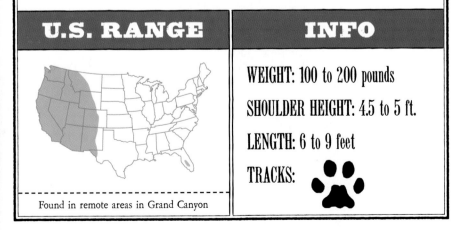

Found in remote areas in Grand Canyon

INFO

WEIGHT: 100 to 200 pounds

SHOULDER HEIGHT: 4.5 to 5 ft.

LENGTH: 6 to 9 feet

TRACKS:

MULE DEER

Odocoileus hemionus

Mule deer are the most commonly spotted large mammal in the park. Although closely related to white-tailed deer, mule deer are slightly larger and have white tails with a black tip. Mule deer are found predominantly in mountainous areas of the arid Southwest. They are named for their large ears that move independently of each other—like mule ears. Bucks grow antlers that are shed each winter. Although conflict between bucks is infrequent, mild fights sometimes break out where antlers are enmeshed while each buck tries to force the head of the other down. Injuries are rare, but if the antlers become locked both bucks will be unable to feed, and both will ultimately die of starvation. Fights between does are much more common, and as a result family groups tend to be spaced widely apart. Young does give birth to one fawn, but older does often give birth to twins. Fawns are able to distinguish their mother from other does through a unique odor produced by glands on the mother's hind legs.

U.S. RANGE

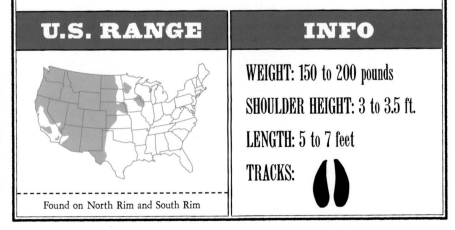

Found on North Rim and South Rim

INFO

WEIGHT: 150 to 200 pounds

SHOULDER HEIGHT: 3 to 3.5 ft.

LENGTH: 5 to 7 feet

TRACKS:

PEREGRINE FALCON

Falco peregrinus

Peregrine falcons are birds of prey that can spot victims from thousands of feet above. Once a target is selected, the peregrine dive bombs it at speeds topping 200 mph. The collision creates an explosion of feathers, and victims that don't die immediately upon impact have their necks broken by the peregrine's specially designed beak. Peregrines are such successful strikers that they were used to kill Nazi carrier pigeons in World War II. By the early 1970s, however, peregrine falcons were at the brink of extinction. The extinction of the passenger pigeon (an important source of food) and the toxic effects of the pesticide DDT had reduced the worldwide population to less than 40 pairs. To save the remaining birds, young peregrines were raised in captivity and released in the wild. The program has been remarkably successful. In 1999 peregrines were removed from the federal Endangered Species List. There are currently over 1,650 breeding pairs in the United States and Canada.

U.S. RANGE

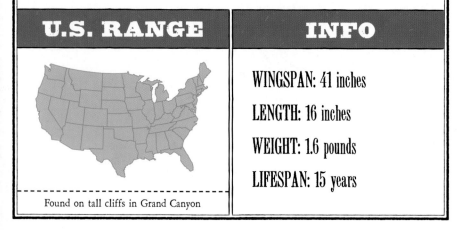

Found on tall cliffs in Grand Canyon

INFO

WINGSPAN: 41 inches

LENGTH: 16 inches

WEIGHT: 1.6 pounds

LIFESPAN: 15 years

RATTLESNAKES

Crotalus scutulatus (below), Crotalus viridis abyssus (right)

There are six species of rattlesnakes in Grand Canyon, including the Mojave Rattlesnake (above) and Grand Canyon Rattlesnake (right). Rattlesnakes are the only venomous snakes in the Canyon. Although they have poor eyesight, they have a sharp sense of smell and can detect body heat through infrared sensors located on either side of their head. Their keen senses are used to detect prey while a rattler lies in wait. When the rattler strikes, it injects a paralyzing venom through sharp fangs. Once the victim is motionless, the rattler swallows it whole. Rattlers, in turn, are preyed upon by coyotes, eagles, and hawks. Hawks pluck rattlers from the ground, then drop them repeatedly from the air until the rattler is dead. The Inner Grand Canyon is the only place in the world where the Grand Canyon Rattlesnake, a subspecies of the Western Rattlesnake, is found. It evolved over millions of years in the confines of the Canyon. The Grand Canyon Rattler is distinguished by its pale, pinkish coloration, and irregular dark blotches that become paler toward the center.

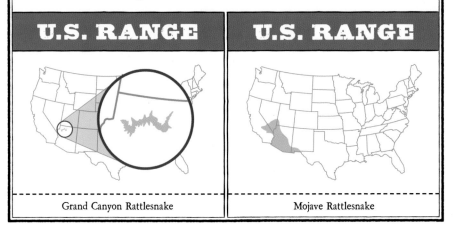

U.S. RANGE	U.S. RANGE
Grand Canyon Rattlesnake	Mojave Rattlesnake

HUMPBACK CHUB

Gila cypha

The humpback chub is Grand Canyon's most famous native fish. It first appeared 3–5 million years ago in the whitewater-filled canyons of the Colorado River Basin. Because it evolved in swift muddy waters, the chub developed remarkable biological adaptations. Large fins allow it to easily maneuver rapids. Small eyes protect it from silt. And when swift water passes over its pronounced hump, the chub is forced down toward the bottom of the river where the current is less strong, helping it stay put during floods. Humpback chub thrived in the virgin Colorado, but the species is now on the verge of extinction due to dams, which have significantly lowered water temperatures in the river. Although chubs can survive in cold water, they need warm water to spawn. Today they are forced to spawn in a handful of smaller tributaries. The new Colorado has also allowed non-native species such as trout to thrive, competing for resources and feeding on young chub. Although scattered chub populations exist above Lake Powell, the largest remaining chub population (less than 2,000 fish) lives in Grand Canyon near the junction of the Little Colorado River.

U.S. RANGE

* Historic Range

Found only in Colorado River Basin

INFO

LENGTH: 18 inches

WEIGHT: 2 pounds

COLOR: Green, Silver, White

LIFESPAN: 30 years

RAINBOW TROUT

Oncorhynchus mykiss

Rainbow trout are one of the world's most prized sport fish. They have an olive/bluish back and a characteristic pink band running down their sides. Although they are native to rivers in the western United States, rainbow trout are extremely adaptable. Over the past century they have been transplanted to rivers in Africa, Japan, Southeast Asia, South America, Europe, Australia, and New Zealand. Rainbow trout were introduced to the Colorado River just north of the Grand Canyon following the completion of Glen Canyon Dam in 1964. The cool, clear water released from the bottom of the dam created ideal trout habitat, and after it was stocked it became a world-famous fishery. Unfortunately, some of the trout have found their way downstream to the confluence of the Colorado River and the Little Colorado River—a vital spawning ground for native fish. To prevent trout from feeding on young native fish, federal employees have instituted an aggressive trout removal policy. Trout are shocked with electro-fishing gear, captured, and euthanized. The carcasses are then given to local Indians for use as fertilizer.

U.S. RANGE

INFO

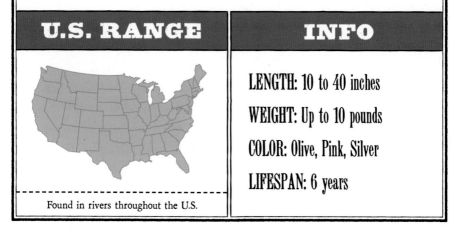

Found in rivers throughout the U.S.

LENGTH: 10 to 40 inches

WEIGHT: Up to 10 pounds

COLOR: Olive, Pink, Silver

LIFESPAN: 6 years

HISTORY

HUMANS FIRST SET eyes on Grand Canyon roughly 10,000 years ago, when primitive hunters and gatherers first arrived in Arizona. Little is known about these prehistoric people, but small artifacts found in the backs of caves confirm their existence in Grand Canyon. Among the objects discovered were spear points and small split-twig figurines twisted into the shapes of animals. Some of the animal figurines were pierced with tiny spears made of agave thorns, indicating that hunting played an important role in their lives.

What ultimately happened to these early settlers is unclear. It's possible that they abandoned Grand Canyon, but it's just as likely that they stayed. In either case, a new culture called the Ancestral Puebloans (Anasazi) appeared several thousand years later. The Ancestral Puebloans occupied the Four Corners region from roughly A.D. 0 to 1200, and for over a thousand years they flourished in Grand Canyon, which marked the westernmost range of their territory.

Archaeologists have subdivided the Ancestral Puebloans into two distinct cultural groups: the Basketmakers and the Pueblo Anasazi. The Basketmakers lived from A.D. 0 to 700. Named for their exceptional skill at basketry, they wove plant fibers into beautiful baskets and sandals. Because they were hunter-gatherers the Basketmakers were constantly on the move in search of food, but as time passed they discovered agriculture, which allowed them to settle down in one place. They constructed dwellings in caves or under overhanging cliffs, and they grew beans, corn and squash nearby.

Although farming was the Basketmakers' main source of food, they also hunted animals with spears, which provided them with food and raw materials for clothing. In the winter Basketmakers wore robes made of deer skin, rabbit skin, or turkey feathers. In the summer they wore loin clothes and skirts woven from plant fibers. Jewelry was made from seashells imported along trade routes from the Pacific Coast, and live parrots were imported from Mexico. The Basketmakers kept dogs as pets, smoked tobacco from pipes, and played music on six-hole flutes. By A.D. 600 they had also learned to make pottery.

Split-twig figurine

Around A.D. 700 the Basketmakers discovered the bow and arrow, which allowed them to hunt more food in less time. With more free time on their hands they continued to advance technologically, and soon they were using stone masonry to build impressive stone villages under the awnings of cliffs. Some of these dwellings, such as Canyon de Chelly in northeast Arizona and Chaco Canyon in New Mexico, are among of the most spectacular archaeological ruins in America.

As Ancestral Puebloan lifestyles advanced, so did the rules governing their society. Customs and social codes became highly developed, with some villages operating like independent city-states. Archaeologists consider these later Ancestral Puebloans part of the second cultural group: the Pueblo Anasazi.

The Pueblo Anasazi built irrigation ditches near fertile areas and stored surplus crops in granaries (stone storage compartments). Artistic achievements also blossomed during this time. Cotton was spun and woven into beautiful clothes, dwellings were covered with murals and pictographs, and elaborate costumes were used in religious ceremonies. By A.D. 1100 the Ancestral Puebloans were flourishing, occupying thousands of sites in and around Grand Canyon. Their technological achievements were extraordinary, placing them among the most advanced Indians north of Mexico. Then, at the height of their prosperity, the Ancestral Puebloans mysteriously abandoned their settlements and vanished from Grand Canyon.

Archaeologists are at a loss to explain the swift departure of the Ancestral Puebloans. Some believe they fell victim to a massive drought. Others blame a depletion of natural resources. Still others think there was a great war between neighboring tribes. Unfortunately, little evidence remains to provide a clear picture of what actually happened. Whatever the cause, after abandoning Grand Canyon many Ancestral Puebloans moved south and merged with the Hopi and Zuni tribes. Within a few centuries, other tribes including the Havasupai, Hualapai, Southern Paiute, and Navajo had settled the surrounding territory.

Ancestral Puebloan Pottery

Mystery of the
Ancestral Puebloans

THE SWIFT DECLINE of the Ancestral Puebloans is one of the Southwest's greatest archaeological mysteries. Why would a culture at the height of its prosperity—by many accounts the most advanced culture north of Mexico—suddenly abandon its settlements? What caused them to flee the Four Corners region they had occupied for over 1,000 years, never to return?

For decades archaeologists believed the Ancestral Puebloans fell victim to a massive drought. The entire Southwest experienced a period of decreased rainfall in the late 1200s, and it seemed logical to connect this drought to the ancient culture's demise. But recent evidence suggests the so-called Great Drought may not have been enough to cause a complete cultural collapse. The Ancestral Puebloans, it turns out, started to abandon their settlements prior to the drought. And they had survived worse droughts in the past. Why should this one be different?

Some archaeologists believe the abandonment was triggered by a depletion of the region's scarce natural resources, which could have led to social and political upheaval—possibly even war. In fact, many Ancestral Puebloan structures built near the end appear to be defensive in nature. But if there was a war, why didn't the winners stay to enjoy the spoils?

Some archaeologists believe the demise of the Ancestral Puebloans was triggered by a religious collapse. Religion and daily life were one and the same to the Ancestral Puebloans, and a collapse of one could have led to a collapse of the other. Faced with failing crops, chronic shortages, and rain dances that no longer worked, the Ancestral Puebloans may have lost faith in their prevailing religion. At the same time, the Hopi's new Katsina religion was gaining momentum to the south. With its colored masks and lurid dances, the Katsina movement may have lured the Ancestral Puebloans away from their homeland. A few archaeologists have speculated that some Ancestral Puebloans may have moved as far away as Mexico.

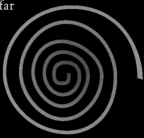

While these theories offer possible explanations, many unanswered questions remain. Until new evidence comes to light, the Ancestral Puebloans' abandonment will continue to be one of Grand Canyon's best-kept secrets.

Arizona Tribes

HOPI

The Hopi are one of the oldest tribes in the region, having lived in northeast Arizona for over 1,000 years. Oraibi, a Hopi village 80 miles east of Grand Canyon, was settled over 800 years ago, making it the oldest continuously inhabited town in the United States. Grand Canyon is a deeply symbolic place for the Hopi, who believe that both people and animals emerged from the Grand Canyon at a place called the *Sipapuni*, a mineral spring located near the junction of the Colorado and Little Colorado Rivers. Hopi religion revolves around *Katsinas*, spirit beings who visit Hopi villages for a few months each year, performing good deeds, punishing criminals, and bringing rain. The Hopi craft hundreds of brightly painted wooden dolls, called *Tihu*, to represent different Katsinas. Tihu—also called Kachina Dolls—are traditionally carved from a single piece of cottonwood root and given to children to teach them about the different Katsinas.

SOUTHERN PAIUTE

The Southern Paiute settled the plateau country north of Grand Canyon around A.D. 1300. Because of the region's limited resources, they found it easier to exist in small bands rather than large groups governed by complex social structures. Each band had an individual leader who acted as a tribal advisor. The leader was generally an elderly man who had spent a lifetime studying the landscape, and he imparted his knowledge of plants and animals to others. The Southern Paiute hunted deer and small game on the Kaibab Plateau, which encompasses much of Grand Canyon's North Rim. *Kaibab* is derived from a Paiute word meaning "Mountain Lying Down." While the men hunted, the women gathered plants. Over time, the Southern Paiute also adopted agriculture from the nearby Hopi and Navajo tribes.

HAVASUPAI

The Havasupai have been living in western Grand Canyon for over 700 years. The name *Havasupai*, "People of the Blue-Green Water," is a reference to the beautiful turquoise pools and waterfalls found in Havasu Canyon. Because the Havasupai had access to constant water, they grew more food than any other tribe in the region. Havasu Creek, one of the most dependable water sources in Grand Canyon, helped the Havasupai weather even the greatest droughts.

The *Hualapai*, "Pine Tree People," were close neighbors of the Havasupai. Although listed as two separate tribes by early American explorers, the Havasupai and Hualapai consider themselves members of the same *Pai* culture. The Hualapai spent most of their time in the forested plateaus above Grand Canyon, but in the summer they would sometimes gather plants in the rugged side canyons along the South Rim.

NAVAJO

The Navajo were one of the last tribes to settle the Grand Canyon region, arriving from northwest Canada sometime between 500 and 1,000 years ago. Upon reaching the desert they were forced to adopt a new way of life. Unable to survive on their own, they resorted to raiding the villages of previously settled tribes. Eventually, however, they learned agriculture from their neighbors. Traditional Navajo homes are called *hogans*, one-room buildings built out of logs and tree branches that always face east so the Navajo can start each day by greeting the light of the rising sun. The Navajo believe that humans must live in harmony with nature, achieving a sense of place called *hozho*. They refer to themselves *Dine*, "The People." In the 1600s Spaniards introduced sheep to the Navajo, and before long Navajo culture revolved around sheep herding. Sheep meat replaced deer meat as the primary source of protein in the Navajo diet, and sheep wool was woven into beautiful rugs with colorful designs. Navajo legend speaks of two animal beings, Spider Man and Spider Woman, who taught the Navajo how to build looms and weave.

Coronado expedition

A FABLED CITY OF GOLD

L ESS THAN 30 years after Columbus discovered North America, Spanish conquistador Hernán Cortéz defeated the Aztecs in Mexico. At the time Spain was the most powerful country in the world. Its sprawling empire covered much of Europe and stretched across the Atlantic. But maintaining these far-flung properties was an expensive proposition, and despite the vast wealth plundered from the Aztecs, Spain was soon desperate for additional funds.

In 1529 a Spanish vessel shipwrecked off the Texas coast. The wreck's four survivors spent the next seven years wandering the desert, and when they finally returned to Mexico they told stories of a fabulous city of gold located somewhere in the American Southwest. This city, referred to as the Seven Cities of Cibola, quickly captured the imagination of the Spanish crown.

In 1540 Spanish authorities organized a military expedition to locate the Seven Cities of Cibola. Led by charismatic, 29-year-old Francisco Vásquez de Coronado, the expedition consisted of 300 Spanish men, several hundred Indians, and thousands of cattle, sheep, and goats. Five months later the expedition reached the spot where the Seven Cities were rumored to be located. All they found was a small Indian village.

Coronado was dejected, but the Indians told him of a larger group of seven cities to the west. Coronado immediately dispatched his lieutenant, Don Pedro de Tovar, to investigate these claims. When Tovar returned he reported that he had failed to locate the Seven Cites of Cibola, but he had learned of a mighty river to the west. Hoping this river was the gateway to Cibola, Coronado dispatched another search party under the command of García López de Cárdenas.

After three weeks of harrowing travel, Cárdenas' party became the first Europeans to set eyes on Grand Canyon. But they were hardly impressed by what they saw. From their vantage point on the South Rim—believed to be somewhere between Moran Point and Desert View—the Spaniards estimated that the Colorado River was just six feet wide. (In fact, the average width of the Colorado in Grand Canyon is closer to 300 feet.) Although their Hopi guides insisted that the river was much larger, the Spaniards refused to believe them. They had never encountered a natural landmark of such scale, and they were unable to comprehend its true dimensions.

For three days the Spaniards tried to find a route to the river. One group of soldiers made it one-third of the way down, but they were unable to descend any farther. Even at that depth, they were shocked to discover rocks taller than the 185-foot tower of Seville in Spain; from the rim the rocks had appeared only a few feet tall. Suddenly comprehending Grand Canyon's true dimensions, Cárdenas turned his men around. Coronado's expedition ultimately traveled as far as present-day Kansas, but the Seven Cities of Cibola were never found.

THE SECOND SPANISH WAVE

N THE DECADES following Coronado's expedition, Spain once again ignored the American Southwest. No colonization attempts were made until 1598, when Juan de Onate founded Santa Fe, New Mexico. Within a few decades, Spanish missions had spread west towards Hopi towns.

The Hopi deeply resented the proselytizing missionaries. They had no interest in changing their religious beliefs, and they did not want the Spaniards interfering in their daily lives. Before long Indian mistrust reached a breaking point. In 1680 leaders from several tribes met in secret to plan a coordinated revolt against the Spanish. The Pueblo Revolt, as it was later called, drove out the Spanish and allowed the Indians to regain control of their territories. But their victory was short-lived. Twelve years later a more powerful Spanish army marched north to reconquer the Southwest. As the army approached, the Hopi retreated to the tops of tall mesas, which were easily defended from above. Hopi mesas soon became a favored refuge for Indians fleeing the Spanish throughout the Southwest.

While battles raged to the east of Grand Canyon, Indians living in the remote western Grand Canyon remained relatively undisturbed. Then, in 1776, a Franciscan missionary named Francisco Tomás Garcés attempted to blaze a trail between the Spanish missions in California and the missions along the Rio Grande. His journey led him up the Colorado River into western Grand Canyon, where he encountered the Havasupai Indians. The Havasupai graciously invited Garcés to stay for five days of feasting—an offer that he gladly accepted. When the feast was over, Garcés set out to visit the Hopi villages to the east. But the Hopi, stung by years of warfare, were deeply suspicious of the Spaniard. They refused to feed Garcés or even accept his gifts. Taking the hint, Garcés returned to Havasu Canyon, where he was greeted with another multi-day feast.

Not long after Garcés' journey, another Spanish expedition, the Dominguez-Escalante party, left New Mexico to find a northern route to the Pacific. By the time they reached the Sierra Nevada Mountains, however, deep snows had already set in and the mountains were impassable. Forced to abandon their mission, the Spaniards headed south, at one point crossing the Colorado River near the northern tip of Grand Canyon. The Dominguez-Escalante party became the third and final Spanish expedition to set eyes on Grand Canyon.

Although the Spanish had relatively little contact with Indians living near Grand Canyon, their indirect presence had a huge impact on Indian life. The Spanish introduced horses, cattle, and sheep to North America—animals that would come to define many Southwestern tribes—as well as new fruits such as peaches, melons, and figs. But along with these positive influences came deadly diseases such as smallpox, which had a devastating impact on Indian populations throughout the Southwest.

Indian pueblo

AMERICAN EXPLORERS

IN 1821 MEXICO gained independence from Spain and acquired much of the American Southwest. But Mexico, like Spain, generally avoided the desolate region, and Indians living near Grand Canyon remained relatively undisturbed. But a new power was looming on the eastern horizon.

Following the Louisiana Purchase in 1803, American beaver trappers began fanning out across the West. Soon they were scouring the wild streams that tumbled down from the Rockies into the Four Corners region. But even then Grand Canyon was generally avoided as a destination. Although beavers lived at the bottom of the Canyon, reaching them proved too arduous a task.

Not that some trappers didn't try. In 1826 a trapping party led by Ewing Young traveled up the Colorado River on foot. They became the first Americans to set eyes on Grand Canyon, but their journey was a miserable one. At one point the men plodded through 18 inches of snow and ate bark to fend off starvation. Not surprisingly, they found little to like about the region. As one of the trappers, James Pattie, remembered, "We arrived where the river emerges from these horrid mountains, which so cage it up, as to deprive all human beings of the ability to descend to its banks, and make use of its waters."

Such descriptions did little to encourage further exploration. With its extreme climate, physically challenging terrain, and striking lack of water, the Four Corners region was a terrible place to settle—which was precisely why Mormon leader Brigham Young decided to settle there.

THE ILL-FATED EXPLORER

IN 1857 THE U.S. War Department sent novice Lieutenant Joseph Ives on an expedition to explore the lower reaches of the Colorado River. Unfortunately for Ives, the expedition's 50-foot steamboat, *The Explorer*, was poorly designed to handle the rapids, shallows, and sand bars of the Colorado. The boat ran aground countless times, and the crew was often forced to unload and tow the boat by hand. After two months of slow progress and much towing, *The Explorer* struck a boulder near the present site of Hoover Dam. The crew was tossed overboard and the boat was wrecked beyond repair.

Defeated, Ives declared that he had reached the farthest point of navigation on the river. Not only was his statement untrue, Ives had already been proven wrong. Several weeks earlier a man named George Johnson, incensed at being passed over by the War Department to lead the historic journey, had steamed his own boat past the point where *The Explorer* wrecked.

Ives's expedition produced several fine maps of the region, but much of the Colorado River remained a mystery. Writing in his log, Ives concluded his journey with the unfortunate remark: "The region is, of course, altogether valueless. It can be approached only from the south, and after entering it there is nothing to do but leave. Ours has been the first, and will doubtless be the last, party of whites to visit this profitless locality."

Today Grand Canyon, Hoover Dam, and nearby Las Vegas attract over 40 million visitors each year.

Fleeing religious persecution in Illinois, Young led his followers to Utah's Great Salt Lake in 1846. The desolate landscape offered the perfect refuge for the Mormons—a place where they could practice their new religion in peace. Over the next two decades, Mormon settlements spread south, representing the first significant white presence anywhere near Grand Canyon. But even the notoriously rugged Mormons refused to explore Grand Canyon's depths. That job would fall to a 34-year-old geology professor named John Wesley Powell.

JOHN WESLEY POWELL

IN 1848, FOLLOWING the conclusion of the Mexican War, the United States acquired the vast chunk of land that would one day make up California, Nevada, Arizona, Utah, Colorado, and New Mexico. But even by the 1860s, maps of the United States had a single word splashed across the Grand Canyon region: UNEXPLORED. Most men, even the heroically rugged trappers who had opened up much of the West, took one look at those maps and stayed away. But one man looked at the maps and saw an opportunity for everlasting fame.

John Wesley Powell was probably the least likely man in America to conquer the Colorado River. A one-armed college professor with virtually no whitewater experience, he was a case study in everything that *wasn't* needed to successfully navigate the river. At five feet six inches tall, he hardly cut an imposing figure. But what Powell lacked in physical stature he more than made up for in personal ambition.

In 1868 Powell decided to organize an expedition to explore the Colorado River and the desolate canyon country it flowed through. He went to Washington, D.C. to raise money for the trip, but with the federal treasury still reeling from the Civil War government funds were hard to come by. Powell was offered

HERO or LIAR?

JAMES WHITE

IN 1867, two years before Powell's expedition, a raft was pulled from the Colorado River just below Grand Canyon. On board was a starving, sunburned, half-naked man named James White, who proceeded to tell a story so amazing that it is still disputed to this day. White claimed to have spent the previous two weeks floating down the Colorado lashed to a raft, making him the first man to successfully run Grand Canyon. Most modern scholars dispute White's story, based mostly on the fact that it's so hard to believe. But supposing it's true, White's journey would have been one of the most remarkable whitewater adventures of all time.

some military rations, however, which he gladly accepted. Undaunted, he ultimately managed to scrape together funding from a variety of private institutions.

Powell's next step was to assemble a crew. The job offered no pay, harsh living conditions, and life-threatening risks. Not surprisingly, the men who accepted these terms were reckless, crazy, or a little of both. Most were trappers and mountain men eager for adventure and excitement. But to Powell, the journey was primarily a scientific expedition. "The object," he wrote, "is to make collections in geology, natural history, antiquities, and ethnology."

On May 24, 1869, Powell's expedition launched four boats from Green River City, Wyoming. Their starting point was 6,100 feet above sea level. Their destination—Grand Wash Cliffs, near present-day Lake Mead—lay at an elevation of 1,300 feet. How the river got there was anyone's guess.

For the first week of their journey the men floated peacefully down the Green River. The one-armed Powell, unable to row, sat perched on a chair tied to his boat. At first the lazy current bored the men, but soon the river started to intensify. As they continued downstream, the rapids became frequent and fierce. Then on June 9, one of the boats slipped into a large rapid before the crew had a chance to scout it. The boat plunged into the whitewater and smashed on a rock, splintering into pieces. The three men onboard managed to swim to safety, but a third of the expedition's supplies were lost.

rescue by

IN DESOLATION Canyon, Powell and a crew member named George Bradley set out to climb the steep cliffs above the river. As the one-armed Powell neared the top he became stranded on the edge of a cliff. "Standing on my toes my muscles began to tremble," he wrote. "If I lose my hold I shall fall to the bottom." Powell called to Bradley, who quickly appeared on a ledge above. With time running out, Bradley stripped off his long johns and lowered them down, but they dangled behind Powell just out of reach. Taking a deep breath, Powell leaned back into space and grabbed for the long johns with his one good hand. Catching a pant leg, Powell held on for dear life while Bradley hauled him up to safety.

Disaster Falls

Powell expedition boats

Following Disaster Falls (as Powell later named it) a nervous energy settled over the crew. They were only two weeks into their journey, and they had already lost one of their boats. What would happen if they lost another? The rapids were growing worse, and soon they would be hundreds of miles from civilization.

Determined, the men carried on. For the next two months they followed the Green River as it passed through Wyoming and Utah, running rapids whenever they could but spending most of their time lining or portaging. Lining involved guiding the boats downstream as the men held on to ropes from the shore. It was excruciating work. The ropes burned the men's hands and they were constantly slipping on wet rocks. The alternative was portaging, which entailed carrying the boats—and several thousand pounds of supplies—on shore past the rapid.

By the time the expedition reached the confluence of the Green River and the Grand River (the official start of the Colorado), supplies were running low. They were down to several pounds of spoiled bacon, a few sacks of flour, and some dried apples. The men tried to supplement their diet by hunting, but game in the region was scarce. Before long, the constant hunger and backbreaking days were taking a serious toll on group morale.

On August 4 the expedition reached the start of Grand Canyon. Drifting through the Canyon's upper reaches, Powell was spellbound by the variety of rocks he saw. He thought the highly polished limestone looked like marble, so he named the initial stretch Marble Canyon. Soon the cliffs rose thousands of feet on either side. The scale of the canyon was breathtaking. "We are three quarters of a mile in the depths of the Earth," Powell wrote, "and the great river shrinks into insignificance, as it dashes its angry waves against the walls and cliffs, that rise to the world above; they are but puny ripples, and we are but pygmies."

While Powell marveled at the natural spectacle, many of the crew felt confined. The Canyon was like a prison to them. Daytime highs topped 100°F and the rapids were frequent and fierce. Before long, many began to openly regret their decision to come.

Continuing on, the men twisted deep in the heart of the Canyon. Soon they were fighting off rapids the size of three-story buildings. Even worse, they had no idea what to expect around each bend in the river. There were rumors of giant waterfalls in Grand Canyon, and if those rumors proved true the expedition would find itself trapped at the bottom of a mile deep chasm. Physically and mentally, the men were starting to unwind. They were now down to starvation rations and the threat of death was very real.

On August 27 the men were camped above their worst rapid yet. Many in the group doubted they could run it and survive. That night at dinner, a man named Oramel Howland took Powell aside. Howland told Powell that he and two others were abandoning the expedition. They would take their chances climbing out of the Canyon—a decision that carried equally lethal implications.

Powell respected the men's decision, but he was convinced the rapid could be run. And according to his calculations, the group was no more than 50 miles from the end of their journey. He spent all night trying to convince the men not to leave, but they had seen enough. The three men left the following morning. They were never seen again.

Concentrating on the matter at hand, Powell studied the rapid. The river was hemmed in by steep cliffs, so there was no possibility of portaging. And other than a small section at the top of the rapid, lining was also out of the question. With a slimmed down crew the men abandoned one of the boats and lined the remaining two boats as far as they could. Then they swooped down into the rapid.

The first boat rushed down a steep wave and was swamped with water. The men pulled for their lives. Soon the waves grew too large to do anything but hold on tight. The boats tossed and turned but somehow managed to stay upright. Before the men knew it, the rapid was behind them. Both boats had survived.

Two days later, Powell's expedition reached the end of its journey. As they approached the confluence of the Colorado and the Virgin River, the men saw several Mormons fishing in the river. The Mormons had been posted there for weeks, under orders from Brigham Young to keep their eyes out "for any fragments or relics of [Powell's] party that might drift down the stream." They were shocked to see Powell and his men alive.

The hearts of the skeletal river runners were filled with joy. The Mormons cooked them a meal, and as one crew member recalled, "we laid our dignified manners aside and assumed the manner of so many hogs. Ate as long as we could and went to sleep to wake up hungry." After 99 days on the river, their voyage was finally over.

Powell's death-defying expedition is virtually impossible to imagine today. River guides who have spent decades rowing the modern, dam-controlled Colorado simply shake their heads in awe when asked about Powell's historic journey. His under-supplied, ragtag collection of mountain men conquered the wildest, most unpredictable river in North America. Today their journey is often referred to the last great expedition of the American West.

John Wesley Powell

JOHN WESLEY POWELL'S Colorado River expedition was one of the greatest adventures in American history. But nearly as remarkable as the expedition is the man who organized it all.

John Wesley Powell was born in 1834, the son of a poor itinerant preacher who moved his family across the frontier. As a young man Powell was constantly on the go, enrolling in several different colleges but never staying around long enough to graduate from any of them. When the Civil War broke out, Powell enlisted on the Union side, making Lieutenant within his first two months. At the battle of Shiloh he was shot in his right arm—an injury that required amputation. Refusing to be kept out of the fight, Powell returned to action several months later and accompanied General Sherman on his conquest of Georgia.

Following the war, Powell underwent an operation to ease the constant pain in his amputated arm. The operation failed, and for the rest of his life Powell was plagued with chronic pain from the raw nerve endings at the end of his stump. Not one to dwell on personal misfortune, Powell simply looked to the future as he tried to figure out what to do with his life. "You are a maimed man," his father told him, "Settle down at teaching. It is a noble profession. Get this nonsense of science and adventure out of your mind."

Powell tried to settle down at teaching, but the lure of the West proved too powerful. As a geologist he had led research trips to the headwaters of the Colorado and Green Rivers—two rivers whose waters ultimately flow through Grand Canyon. It was there that Powell developed an obsession with the Southwest. Powell the geologist was convinced that the canyons of the Colorado would give "the best geological section on the continent." Powell the adventurer desperately wanted to be the first to conquer the final frontier of the United States.

And conquer it he did. Following his Grand Canyon expedition, Powell achieved international fame. On the lecture circuit he spoke to packed houses and stayed in the finest hotels. Later, he used his influence to help found the Bureau of American Ethnology and the U.S. Geological Survey.

Powell died in 1902. Shortly before his death, he made an unusual bet with his friend W. J. McGee, president of the National Geographic Society. Although physically smaller than McGee, Powell was convinced his brain was larger. To settle the dispute, the men left instructions to have their brains weighed following their deaths. At 1,488 grams, Powell's brain was five percent heavier. Today it rests in a jar at the Smithsonian Institute.

EARLY SETTLERS

J OHN WESLEY POWELL'S journey inaugurated a wave of expeditions to map and explore Grand Canyon. Leading this charge was Powell himself. Shortly after his historic near-death, near-mutiny expedition, Powell announced plans to lead a second trip down the Colorado. Many of his scientific notes had been lost on the first journey, and he was determined to fill in the blanks. This time, however, he would break his trip into stages with supply points along the way, significantly reducing the risks involved. And so in 1871, the indefatigable Powell conquered the Colorado yet again.

Between river trips Powell conducted scientific expeditions along the rim, but these excursions were only temporary. The region as a whole remained largely uninhabited. Following the arrival of the railroad in northern Arizona in the early 1880s, however, a handful of drifters started taking up permanent residence along the South Rim.

Most of the South Rim's early settlers were miners searching for riches in the depths of Grand Canyon. Although a number of potential mining sites were located, the costs of excavation soon proved prohibitively expensive. Ore had to be packed out on burros, water was scarce, and the closest railroad was two days away. Mining Grand Canyon, it tuned out, was an extremely *un*profitable endeavor. But just as that realization started to sink in, the miners discovered another source of revenue: tourists.

Starting in the mid-1880s, people began arriving at Grand Canyon for no other reason than to visit, relax, and take in the views. This was a strikingly new concept. For hundreds of years Grand Canyon had been avoided—even detested—as a destination. Now, people thought it was beautiful. It was an idea that would turn out to be highly contagious.

The first tourists arrived at the South Rim in 1884 and stayed in makeshift lodges built by miners. Most visitors arrived by stagecoach from the nearby towns of Flagstaff, Williams, and Ash Fork. But the journey was a rugged one. The dirt roads were filled with potholes, and the trip often required at least two days of bone-jarring travel.

It wasn't long before people began looking for a better form of transportation to the South Rim. In 1885 Grand Canyon entrepreneur Bill Bass lured a railroad agent to his lodge to try to convince him of the potential of a spur line to the South Rim. The agent was hardly impressed by what he saw. "No one," he wrote to his superiors, "would go that far only to see a hole in the ground."

It would take over a decade for the railroads to realize their mistake. When they finally did, the previously isolated Grand Canyon would find itself linked directly to the modern world—and visitors would arrive by the thousands.

GRAND CANYON PIONEERS

JOHN HANCE

JOHN HANCE was the first permanent white settler in Grand Canyon. After visiting on a prospecting trip in 1881, he fell in love with the scenery. Two years later he built a log cabin east of Grandview Point and started renting out rooms to guests.

Hance is fondly remembered as Grand Canyon's premier storyteller, but his stories rarely contained a shred of truth. He took great pleasure in spinning tall tales with a deadpan delivery until his hapless listeners realized they'd been had. When Hance was once asked how the Canyon formed, he responded, "It was hard work, took a long time, but I dug it myself, with a pick and a shovel. If you want to know what I done with the dirt, just look south through a clearin' in the trees at what they call the San Francisco Peaks." Hance had hundreds of stories in his repertoire, and he never told the same story twice in exactly the same way.

As Hance once confided to a friend, "I've got to tell stories to them people for their money; and if I don't tell it to them, who will? I can make these tenderfeet believe that a frog eats boiled eggs; and I'm going to do it; and I'm going to make 'em believe that he carries it a mile to find a rock to crack it on."

The tenderfeet loved it. According to one early visitor, "Anyone who comes to the Grand Canyon and fails to meet John Hance will miss half the show." In 1906 he was offered free room and board at the Bright Angel Lodge in exchange for just hanging out with the guests and being himself.

JOHN D. LEE

BEFORE HE was banished to the Grand Canyon by Brigham Young, John D. Lee had been a prosperous Mormon living in southern Utah with his 19 wives. But in 1857 Lee participated in the Mountain Meadow Massacre, in which a group of Mormons slaughtered a wagon train of 120 pioneers on their way to California. In a blatant cover up, the Mormon Church placed the blame solely on Lee's shoulders. With the law at his back, Lee fled to Grand Canyon.

Lee arrived at a spot along the Colorado River just south of present-day Lake Powell and established Lees Ferry. It was the only viable river crossing for hundreds of miles. But being a wanted man and owning the only ferry crossing for hundreds of miles turned out to be a dangerous combination. In 1874 the law finally caught up with Lee, and he was tried and executed. He was survived by his 53 children.

BILL BASS

BILL BASS moved to Williams, Arizona from New Jersey in 1883. Several years later, curiosity and prospecting brought him to the South Rim, where he spent the next 41 years of his life.

Bass came to Grand Canyon to prospect, but he soon turned to tourism as his main source of income. He built a crude tent camp along the South Rim, and he promoted the camp through home-made lantern slides that were displayed throughout the country.

In 1894 Bass guided a young woman named Ada Diefendorf to the beautiful waterfalls in Havasu Canyon. A short while later, Bill and Ada were married, and Ada became the first white woman to raise a family on the South Rim. But life in Grand Canyon was never easy. In addition to household duties such as cooking and cleaning, Ada wrangled horses, cared for livestock, and hiked three days to do laundry in the Colorado River.

In 1926, at the age of 77, Bass sold the claims to his land holdings and retired to Wickenburg, Arizona. By the time he left, he had built more roads and Inner Canyon trails than any other individual in Grand Canyon history.

THE RAILROAD ARRIVES

MINERS AT THE rim weren't the only ones interested in a railroad to Grand Canyon. The nearby towns of Flagstaff and Williams also realized the benefits that a railroad would bring—namely increased tourist dollars—and both towns were soon engaged in a feverish competition to build one. Flagstaff envisioned a railroad supported by tourism. The town's leading citizens pitched their idea to a number of established railroad companies, but as Bill Bass had already discovered the railroads failed to grasp Grand Canyon's tourist potential.

Williams took a different approach. It appealed to mining companies who needed a cheap way to haul ore from their mines located near the South Rim. Mining operations would be the driving force for the new railroad, with tourist dollars providing additional revenue. It was a shrewd pitch, and in 1897 the Santa Fe and Grand Canyon Railway Company was incorporated to build a railroad connecting Williams to the South Rim.

Four years later the railroad reached Grand Canyon Village. By that time, however, the mines that prompted its construction had already been shut down. It hardly mattered. For $3.95 passengers could enjoy a smooth, four-hour train ride to the South Rim instead of a $20, bouncing, all-day stage ride—previously the only option. The result was predictable: tourism boomed.

Visitors arrived by the thousands. The railroad flourished, and before long the price of land near Grand Canyon Village had skyrocketed. A few cunning locals staked bogus mining claims along the South Rim, giving them the questionable right to develop the land. Although the practice was ultimately ruled illegal, a few citizens—most notably Ralph Cameron (p.94)—became very rich off the scheme.

The Santa Fe Railroad owned most of the land surrounding its tracks, giving it a strategic advantage in the local real estate game. To accommodate the flood of new visitors, the railroad built the extravagant El Tovar hotel in Grand Canyon Village. Early settlers who had built hotels away from Grand Canyon Village soon found it hard to compete. Within a decade, most locally owned hotels had shut down.

Life on the rim was changing fast. Just three months after the first train pulled up to the South Rim, the first automobile arrived. Its driver had departed from Flagstaff several days earlier amid much fanfare—but the car broke down soon after it left. Several days later the automobile arrived at the South Rim pulled by a team of mules. The trip was hardly a bad omen. Over the next three decades automobiles would become the most popular form of transportation to Grand Canyon, ultimately forcing the railroad out of business.

While the South Rim buzzed with tourist activity, the North Rim remained as isolated as ever. No railroads came within 100 miles of the North Rim, and settlement was scare. Because of its extreme isolation, the Arizona Strip—the narrow stretch of land between the North Rim and Utah—was a lawless area that attracted a strange mix of cattle thieves, renegades, and Mormons who continued to practice polygamy. Although Utah tried several times to annex the Arizona Strip, citing Arizona's poor law enforcement as a primary concern, Arizona was able to retain control of the land.

Due to its remote location, the North Rim was filled with wild game, a fact that soon attracted hunting parties. North Rim sport hunting got off to a rocky start, however, when a man named John Young attempted to build a hunting lodge that would cater to British aristocrats. Young contacted Buffalo Bill Cody, who was then performing in England, and convinced him to round up a group of potential investors. When the eager Britons arrived later that year, they took one look at the desolate landscape and hightailed it back to England.

American hunters, on the other hand, were more than happy to venture to the rugged North Rim, and sport hunting soon flourished. In 1906 Congress established Grand Canyon Game Reserve, which included much of the North Rim. A few years later ex-President Theodore Roosevelt visited the North Rim on a hunting trip. Starting from the South Rim, he descended the Bright Angel trail and boarded a metal cage that shuttled passengers across the river via a cable and pulley system. Halfway across the river, one of the cables snapped. The cage jolted violently, but Roosevelt made it safely across. After exiting the cage Roosevelt cried out, "Let's do it again!"

High-profile visits like these focused even greater attention on the region. It soon became clear that Grand Canyon was not just a fly-by-night tourist attraction, but a major national landmark. Many felt it deserved to be recognized as such. Before long, the wheels were in motion to create Grand Canyon National Park.

the LION HUNTER

IN 1906 James "Uncle Jim" Owens was appointed manager of the newly established Grand Canyon Game Reserve. Although the Reserve protected game in Grand Canyon, the legal definition of game did not include predators such as bobcats and mountain lions. In fact, these animals were aggressively hunted to protect "less threatening" game. During his time on the North Rim, Uncle Jim claimed to have shot over 1,200 mountain lions. The walls of his cabin were covered with mountain lion claws, and a sign outside advertised, "Lions Caught to Order, Reasonable Rates." But the widespread extermination of mountain lions led to an explosion in the local deer population—a situation that created many new problems. Ultimately, predator hunting was banned in Grand Canyon to allow predators to keep deer populations in check.

the south rim
SWINDLER

OF ALL THE real estate swindlers who came to Grand Canyon in the late 1800s, none was more successful than Ralph Cameron. Shortly after the arrival of the railroad, Cameron began staking mining claims along the South Rim, and before long he had staked over 13,000 acres. But Cameron had little interest in mining. The claims gave him the right to develop the land, which was much more valuable as commercial real estate.

For his claims to be legal, however, he needed to actually mine the land. Cameron paid little attention to this technicality. He simply "salted" the claims with imported minerals and set up bogus mining equipment. Once his claims were established, Cameron took great pleasure in lording them over the Santa Fe Railroad, who felt *it* had the right to develop the land.

One of Cameron's most contentious claims was located next to the train depot, a spot where he knew the railroad wanted to build a hotel. Cameron built his own hotel there instead. In retaliation, the railroad moved their terminal several hundred feet to the east so train passengers would have to pass the railroad-owned Bright Angel Hotel on their way to Cameron's hotel. Visitation to Cameron's hotel soon plummeted.

But Cameron had one more trick up his sleeve. His "mining" claims also gave him sole control of the Bright Angel Trail, the only trail into the Canyon anywhere near Grand Canyon Village. Acting as tollkeeper, Cameron charged $1 a head for every tourist who wanted to descend the trail on horseback. The railroad filed a lawsuit, but Cameron prevailed in court. In retaliation, the railroad spent thousands of dollars improving the Hermit Trail, located several miles west of the Bright Angel Trail, as an alternative to the Bright Angel Trail. But Cameron, who owned mining claims on the Hermit Trail too, howled at the injustice. Tired of his antics, the railroad relented and paid $40,000 for his bogus claims.

As the years wore on, Cameron lost the will to compete with the railroad. In 1910 he shut down his hotel, but he continued to charge a toll on the Bright Angel Trail. By the time the Park Service finally gained control of the trail, Cameron had leveraged his wealth and power into a seat in the U.S. Senate. For years he continued to fight the park over the legitimacy of his mining claims. It wasn't until 1920 that the Arizona Supreme Court finally invalidated Cameron's claims, ending his once-grand real estate empire.

Grand Canyon

Santa Fe

of Arizona

The California Limited

- the train of luxury -
takes you to the rim of this world-wonder

u may stop at El Tovar Hotel, managed by Fred Harvey

May I send you our art booklets
describing the Canyon and the Limited?
Free on request. Address W.J. Black, Pass Traffic Mgr. A.T.& S.F. Ry. System
1112 Z Railway Exchange Chicago

John Hance & Teddy Roosevelt

Park entrance, 1931

GRAND CANYON NATIONAL PARK

AS EARLY AS 1886, Indiana Senator Benjamin Harrison had introduced legislation to preserve Grand Canyon as a national park. At that time there was only one other national park—Yellowstone, created in 1872—and Harrison's legislation sputtered out due to lack of enthusiasm. Two decades later, when Harrison was President, he used his power to establish "Great Canyon Reserve." It was a victory for Grand Canyon, but many Arizona miners and cattlemen resented the new restrictions placed on the land.

Despite scattered local opposition, there were many who saw the need to protect Grand Canyon. In 1906 the Act for the Preservation of American Antiquities was passed, giving the President the power to set aside areas that held "objects of historic or scientific nature." That same year President Theodore Roosevelt created Grand Canyon Game Reserve. For Roosevelt it was an easy decision. When he had visited Grand Canyon a few years earlier, he proclaimed it to be "the most impressive scenery I have ever looked at."

The creation of Grand Canyon Game Reserve was just the beginning. Two years later Roosevelt established Grand Canyon National Monument—the highest designation a piece of American land can receive without Congressional approval. At that point Arizona was not yet a state, so it had no Senators or Congressmen to champion the creation of a national park. In 1912 Arizona was admitted to the Union, and in 1917 Representative Carl Hayden and Senator Henry Fountain of Arizona introduced legislation to create Grand Canyon National Park. On February 26, 1919, President Woodrow Wilson signed the bill into law.

But creating a national park and running it smoothly were two entirely different matters. Early administrators lacked a coherent vision for the park, and many major infrastructure issues went unresolved. In its first decade of operation, Grand Canyon National Park went through six superintendents. The park needed a strong leader with a long-term commitment to Grand Canyon. It found that leader in Miner Tillotson, a civil engineer who became superintendent in 1927 and occupied the position for over a decade. Through his tireless efforts he helped shape a coherent vision of the park that set the precedent for years to come.

The same year that Tillotson became superintendent, Congress revised the park's boundaries to include a large portion of Kaibab National Forest. Five years later President Herbert Hoover proclaimed a new Grand Canyon National Monument (the old one had become Grand Canyon National Park) that encompassed 300 square miles in western Grand Canyon and an additional 40 miles along the Colorado River.

The park was a success on paper, but the flood of new visitors soon overwhelmed the staff. In its first year as a national park, Grand Canyon received 44,000 visitors. Within a decade, that number rose to nearly 200,000. In 1937, 300,000 arrived. The numbers kept on climbing, but the park's staff remained the same: 10 rangers and one park superintendent. For years the small, dedicated staff worked long hours to accommodate the huge number of visitors. Ultimately, the number of rangers was increased, making the park much more enjoyable for tourists and employees alike.

THE GREAT DAM WARS

BY THE 1960s Grand Canyon seemed to be doing just fine. Its dedicated staff welcomed millions of people from around the world. Movie stars, British royalty, and Arab sheiks all stopped by for a look. The giant hole in the ground that had been avoided for centuries was now one of America's most cherished natural landmarks. Best of all, Grand Canyon's national park status protected it from private development. But a massive *government* project soon threatened to drastically alter the landscape.

In the early 1960s the U.S. Bureau of Reclamation (the government agency responsible for much of the water supply in the West) went looking for a new place to build a dam. Ever since the overwhelming success of Hoover Dam, the Bureau had been constructing massive dams at a frantic rate. The West was grow-

HARPER'S WEEKLY

EDITED BY GEORGE HARVEY

W.H.D.Koerner - '11

ing fast, and it needed water to grow. In the 1930s, '40s, and '50s the Bureau of Reclamation built giant dams wherever it could. Before long, many of the Southwest's most impressive rivers resembled a string of interconnected reservoirs. By the early 1960s there was only one good place left in America to build a giant dam: Grand Canyon.

With its steep walls, deep side canyons, and powerful river, Grand Canyon was the perfect site for a dam. But there was a catch: any reservoir created by a dam would be utterly impractical from a water-use standpoint. The water would have to be pumped out thousands of feet to bring it to civilization, and the costs involved would be prohibitively expensive. But the Bureau of Reclamation wasn't interested in water. It was interested in hydroelectricity. In effect, a dam in Grand Canyon would be nothing more than a giant cash register to fund other, less economically feasible water projects elsewhere. And the Bureau of Reclamation didn't just want one dam in the Grand Canyon. It wanted two.

When conservationists heard the news they went wild. Conservationists detest dams, a fact that became glaringly apparent in 1948 when the Bureau of Reclamation tried to build a dam along the Green River in Echo Park, Utah. The dam would have flooded part of Dinosaur National Monument, and conservationists were loath to let that happen. Led by David Brower of the Sierra Club, they fought tooth and nail to defeat the dam. They succeeded. But their success came at a huge cost.

As part of the compromise to save Dinosaur National Monument, the two sides agreed upon a new dam farther downstream. The site of the new dam was Glen Canyon. Lying just north of Grand Canyon, Glen Canyon was one of the most remote places in the country. Only a few thousand people had ever set eyes upon it. So shortly before Glen Canyon Dam was finished, David Brower—the man who championed its creation—took a river trip through Glen Canyon to see it for himself. He immediately started to cry.

With its gorgeous sandstone arches, fern covered alcoves, and sweeping river views, Glen Canyon was one of the most beautiful places Brower had ever seen. In a few months, it would all be underwater. Brower would later admit

FLOYD DOMINY

"I like Dave Brower, but I don't think he's the sanctified conservationist that so many people think he is. I think he's a selfish preservationist, for the few. Dave Brower hates my guts. Why? Because I've got guts. I've tangled with Dave Brower for many years."

that the creation of Glen Canyon Dam was the greatest failure of his life. From that moment on, he vowed never again to lose another beautiful place to a dam. When Brower found out that the Bureau of Reclamation wanted to build two more dams in the Grand Canyon, he went into overdrive.

Brower was up against stiff competition. The biggest proponent of the new dams was Floyd Dominy, the head of the Bureau of Reclamation. Dominy had spent much of his early career helping struggling Wyoming ranchers build dams to save their families from poverty. He knew firsthand how a lack of water could lead to suffering, and he made it his life's mission to build dams. Dominy's drive and ambition were unprecedented. By the time he became head of the Bureau of Reclamation, he had many powerful allies, including Arizona Senator Carl Hayden, the chairman of the Appropriations Committee.

Brower versus Dominy. Conservation versus economic growth. The battle over the dams in Grand Canyon soon became much more than a battle for Grand Canyon. It became a battle for the future of environmental policy in America. For decades economic development had taken precedent over wilderness. But wilderness was disappearing fast, and many people wanted to preserve what was left before it was too late.

Debate over the dams soon shifted into the public arena. Defending the proposed dams, the Bureau of Reclamation argued that the reservoirs would help tourists enjoy Grand Canyon more fully by allowing them to explore previously inaccessible reaches of the Canyon from motorboats. In response, the Sierra Club took out full-page ads in the *New York Times*, *Los Angeles Times*, *San Francisco Chronicle*, and *Washington Post*. The ads read: "Should we also flood the Sistine Chapel so tourists can get nearer the ceiling?"

The response was overwhelming. Letters protesting the dams arrived at the Bureau of Reclamation in dump trucks. Senators and Congressmen were flooded with requests to save Grand Canyon. The two dams, which would have flooded much of Marble Canyon and the Lower Granite Gorge—including Havasu Creek, one of the most beautiful locations in the Canyon—were stopped dead in their tracks.

DAVID BROWER

"Lake Powell is a drag strip for power boats. It's for people who won't do things except the easy way. The magic of Glen Canyon is dead. It has been vulgarized. Putting water in the Cathedral in the Desert was like urinating on the crypt of St. Peter's."

GRAND CANYON TODAY

ODAY THE BIGGEST challenge facing Grand Canyon is the park's overwhelming number of visitors. In 1956 one million people visited Grand Canyon. Thirteen years later that number doubled. Twenty years later it tripled. To cope with increased traffic and pollution, the park service closed Hermit Road to private vehicles in 1974 and began and offering a free shuttle instead. To deal with overcrowding below the rim, the park instituted a permit and reservation system for overnight camping. Before the permit system it was not unusual for hundreds of people to camp at Phantom Ranch at the bottom of the Canyon—a place that can comfortably accommodate about 90 people.

To cope with increased visitation in the future, the National Park Service drafted a General Management Plan to reduce human impact on the park and keep Grand Canyon in as natural a state as possible. Under the plan, which will be instituted over time, private cars will not be allowed over much of the South Rim and visitors will be shuttled around entirely by bus or a proposed light rail system. Extensive "greenway trails" have also been built along the rim for bikers and pedestrians.

Today over four million people visit Grand Canyon each year. Those numbers are both a blessing and a challenge. But as long as every visitor makes a conscious effort to appreciate and preserve Grand Canyon, it will remain one of the world's great destinations for generations to come.

THE SOUTH RIM

⭐ ⭐ ⭐ ⭐ ⭐

Introduction 107
Map 108
Basics 110
Sights 122
Hiking 172

SOUTH RIM

THE SOUTH RIM, located about 80 miles north of Flagstaff, is what most people think of when they think of Grand Canyon. Here you'll find the park's most famous sights and attractions, as well as the majority of the its lodges, campgrounds, and restaurants.

Because of the South Rim's proximity to Interstate 40, which runs through the towns of Flagstaff and Williams, it's the most accessible part of the park—and therefore the most crowded. During peak summer weekends, some popular viewpoints can feel more like Times Square than the Great Outdoors. But no matter how crowded the South Rim gets, the views are always worth it.

The South Rim is divided into three main areas: Grand Canyon Village (p.120), Hermit Road (p.140), and Desert View Drive (p.156), all of which provide access to dramatic viewpoints and great hikes. To help reduce traffic, the park offers a free shuttle connecting lodges, park buildings, and popular viewpoints in Grand Canyon Village and along Hermit Road. If you want to explore Hermit Road, which offers some of the South Rim's finest viewpoints, you'll have to ride the shuttle between March 1 and November 30, when the road is closed to private vehicle traffic. To explore Desert View Drive, which heads 25 miles east of Grand Canyon Village to Desert View, you can either drive your own car or purchase a ticket for a narrated bus tour (p.116).

Grand Canyon Village is the hub of all tourist activity on the South Rim. Its five lodges—the only ones on the South Rim—accommodate about 1,000 guests, and nearby services including everything from fine dining to auto repair. Grand Canyon Village is also the jumping off point for narrated bus tours and mule trips along popular trails (p.117), as well as the meeting spot for many of the park's excellent, free ranger programs (p.116).

Other than the easy Rim Trail (p.115), which skirts the edge of the Canyon near Grand Canyon Village and Hermit Road, hiking on the South Rim is limited to a handful of trails that drop down the Canyon's steep walls. Hiking from the rim to the Colorado River and back in a single day is very dangerous (some hikers have died in their attempts), but day hikers can still get a sense of the Inner Canyon's beauty by descending only partway down popular trails. The Bright Angel Trail (p.172) is the South Rim's most famous (and crowded) hike, but the South Kaibab Trail (p.180), Hermit Trail (p.186) and Grandview Trail (p.192) offer equally dramatic scenery with fewer crowds.

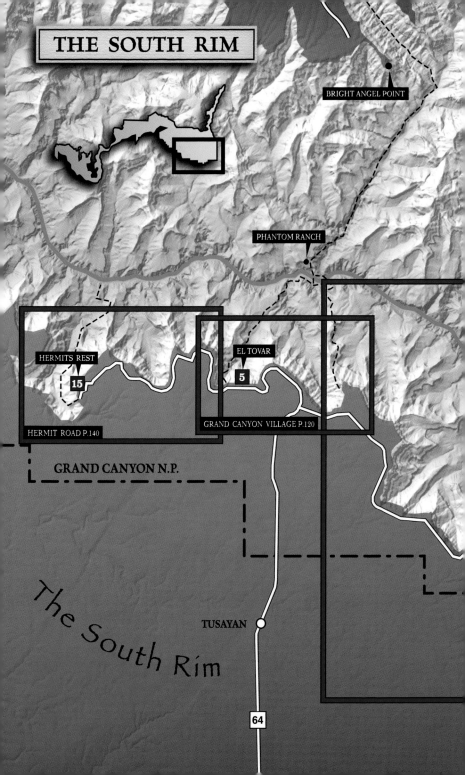

THE SOUTH RIM

BRIGHT ANGEL POINT

PHANTOM RANCH

HERMITS REST

15

EL TOVAR

5

HERMIT ROAD P.140

GRAND CANYON VILLAGE P.120

GRAND CANYON N.P.

The South Rim

TUSAYAN

64

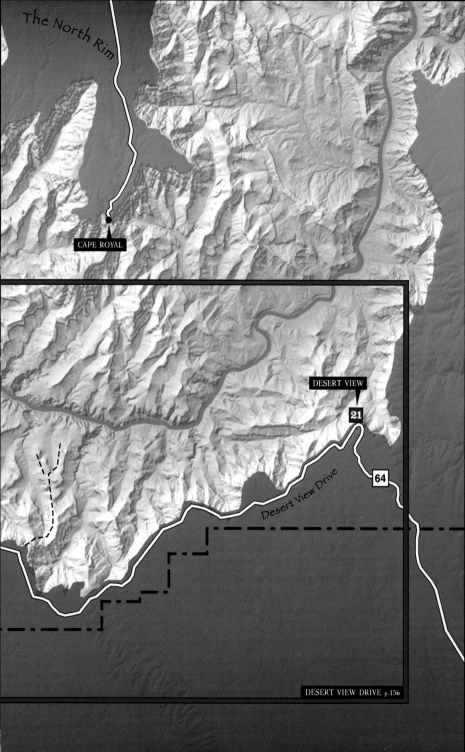

The North Rim

CAPE ROYAL

DESERT VIEW

21

64

Desert View Drive

DESERT VIEW DRIVE p.156

South Rim
BASICS

GETTING TO THE SOUTH RIM

BY CAR

If you're traveling from Flagstaff or Williams, the most direct route to the South Rim heads north on AZ–64, past the small towns of Valle and Tusayan to Grand Canyon's South Entrance Station (about 60 miles from I-80). An alternate route follows US–180 from Flagstaff past the dramatic San Francisco Peaks to Valle, where US–180 merges with AZ-64. If you're driving from northeast Arizona, enter the park via the eastern stretch of AZ–64. From US–89 follow AZ–64 to the East Entrance Station, about 25 miles east of Grand Canyon Village.

BY BUS

Greyhound (800-231-2222, www.greyhound.com) stops in Williams and Flagstaff.

Open Road Tours (800-766-7117, www.openroadtours.com) offers shuttles from the Amtrak station in Flagstaff to Tusayan and Grand Canyon Village. Cost: $25 one-way. Shuttles from Phoenix to Flagstaff are also offered.

BY TRAIN

Amtrak (800-USA-RAIL, www.amtrak.com) runs trains to Williams and Flagstaff.

Grand Canyon Trailway (800-843-8724, www.thetrain.com) offers daily train service from Williams to Grand Canyon Village in vintage railroad cars, some of which are more luxurious (and expensive) than others. The ride lasts about two hours and features mock hold-ups and singing conductors. The train runs throughout the year. Cost: $70–$160.

BY PLANE

The two closest major airports to the South Rim are **McCarran International Airport** in Las Vegas (702-261-5211, www.mccarran.com) and **Phoenix Sky Harbor International Airport** (602-273-3300, www.phxskyharbor.com). Phoenix is about 220 miles from the South Rim and Las Vegas is about 290 miles from the South Rim via major highways. Private planes and charter flights can fly to tiny **Grand Canyon Airport** in Tusayan.

INFORMATION

The best source of seasonal Grand Canyon information—shuttle times, ranger programs, etc.—is the park's free newspaper, *The Guide*. Copies of *The Guide* are available at all park entrance stations, visitor centers, and lodges. There are also ranger-staffed visitor center at Canyon View Information Plaza (p.124) and information desks at Yavapai Observation Station (p.127), Kolb Studio (p.138), Tusayan Museum (p.167), or Desert View (p.170).

WHEN TO GO

The South Rim is open year-round. Summer is by far the most popular time to visit, but the large crowds, hot temperatures, and frequent thunderstorms all combine to make summer a less than ideal time to visit. Scorching midday temperatures in the Inner Canyon also make many of the park's popular hiking trails unbearable in July and August. Despite these inconveniences, the view from the rim remains spectacular—and a late-summer thunderstorm is a sight to behold. Spring and fall offer reduced crowds and much milder temperatures. Spring is also wildflower season, when explosions of color often appear below the rim. Finally there's winter, which brings freezing temperatures, minimal crowds, and reduced rates at park lodges. If you're lucky enough to visit during a snowstorm, you'll witness Grand Canyon at its most beautiful.

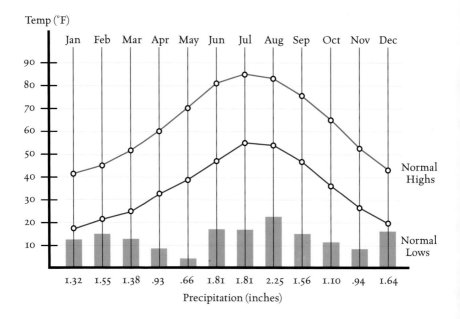

FEES

The North Rim entrance fee (which also gives you access to the South Rim), is $25 per vehicle or $12 per pedestrian, motorcycle rider, or cyclist. Admission is good for seven days. Another option is the America The Beautiful Pass ($80), which gives you unlimited access to all U.S. national parks and federal recreation lands for one full year.

WEATHER

South Rim weather varies dramatically from season to season. Summer is hot—daytime highs often top 80°F—and short afternoon thundershowers sweep through Grand Canyon on a regular basis during monsoon season (July, August, and early September). Winter brings the occasional snowfall, but the snow that falls usually melts within a few days. Spring and fall offer less precipitation and milder temperatures than summer or winter.

WHAT TO BRING

Clothes: No matter when you visit, pack warm clothes—even summer nights can get chilly on the South Rim. Rain gear is also essential during monsoon season in July, August, and early September.

Supplies: Bring supplies for any activities that might interest you (hiking, camping, etc.). If you forget something basic, there's a general store in Grand Canyon Village that carries a wide range of food, camping supplies, and a good selection of outdoor gear.

LODGING

Lodging in Grand Canyon is run by **Xanterra Parks and Resorts** (888-297-2757, www.grandcanyonlodges.com). Rooms fill up fast, so book your reservations as far in advance as possible, *especially* for the busy summer months. Xanterra accepts reservations up to 13 months in advance. Rates listed below are based on the busy summer season. Winter rates are often much cheaper.

BRIGHT ANGEL LODGE & CABINS

This rustic hotel, perched right on the rim of the Canyon, has a bit of a split personality. Its basic rooms (no private bath, showers down the hall) offer some of the best budget lodging in the park, while its well-equipped premium rooms and private cabins feature sweeping Canyon views and working fireplaces.
Rates: $55–$240

EL TOVAR HOTEL

This historic hotel, first opened in 1905, offers the most luxurious lodging in Grand Canyon. If you've got the cash, there's no better place to stay. Perched right on the rim, several rooms at El Tovar have sweeping Canyon views. But all rooms are often booked months in advance. (Also see p.132)
Rates: $145–$325

KACHINA & THUNDERBIRD LODGES

These two identical modern buildings, set about 60 feet back from the rim, are situated between Bright Angel Lodge and El Tovar. Surprisingly, there's not much in the way of Canyon views, but the central location is a definite plus. Both Kachina and Thunderbird offer standard motel-style rooms with two queen beds. Note: Check in at Kachina Lodge is handled by the front desk at El Tovar; check in at Thunderbird Lodge is handled by the front desk at Bright Angel Lodge.
Rates: $140–$155

MASWIK LODGE

Set a quarter-mile back from the rim, Maswik Lodge offers basic motel-style rooms with two queen beds. The lodge is divided into north and south sections (rooms in the north section are more spacious and offer more amenities). In the summer, small rustic cabins are also available. The cabins feature two queen-size (or two double beds) and a private shower
Rates: South section, $80; North Section, $140; Rustic cabins, $80

PHANTOM RANCH

This fantastic collection of rustic buildings, nestled at the bottom of the Canyon along Bright Angel Creek, offers the only overnight lodging below the rim. Accessible by foot or by mule via the Bright Angel Trail or the South Kaibab Trail, Phantom Ranch offers bunkhouses and private cabins that sleep up to four. (Most private cabins are reserved for mule riders on overnight trips, but two hikers' cabins are available). Due to Phantom Ranch's immense popularity, all rooms should be reserved as far in advance as possible. Note: because all food it brought down by mule, all meals must be reserved in advance.
Rates: Bunkhouse, $35; Cabin, $75

YAVAPAI LODGE

Yavapai Lodge is the largest lodge in the park, but because it's situated a half mile from the rim it's less popular than other lodges. That said, it's also the most likely to have rooms on short notice. The lodge offers standard motel-style rooms at Yavapai East (air conditioning) and Yavapai West (ceiling fans).
Rates: Yavapai West, $100; Yavapai East, $125

CAMPING ON THE RIM

DESERT VIEW CAMPGROUND

This campground, located 26 miles east of Grand Canyon Village at Desert View (p.168), is open from mid-May through mid-October. Sites are available on a first-come, first-served basis. Each site accommodates up to six people, three tents, and two vehicles. No RV hook-ups. Cost: $12 per night.

MATHER CAMPGROUND

This large campground, located in Grand Canyon Village, is open year-round. Sites accommodate up to six people, three tents, and two vehicles. (No RV hook-ups, 30-foot maximum vehicle length.) Reservations can be made up to six months in advance and are recommended. Group sites accommodating up to 50 people are also available. For reservations visit www.recreation.gov or call 800-444-6777. Cost: $18; Group sites, $40.

TRAILER VILLAGE

This popular RV campground, located next to Mather Campground and open year-round, offers RV hook-ups and accommodates vehicles up to 50 feet in length. Reservations are highly recommended April–October. Call 888-297-2757 for advance reservations; 928-638-2631 for same-day reservations. Cost: $25.

INNER CANYON CAMPING

Two popular campgrounds, accessible by foot or by mule, are located below the South Rim. Both campgrounds have restrooms and running water. Reservations, issued as permits by the Backcountry Office are essential. See page 19 for more information on Backcountry Permits.

INDIAN GARDEN CAMPGROUND

Located 4.6 miles down the popular Bright Angel Trail, Indian Garden Campground sits above the lush banks of Garden Creek, which supports a thriving population of shady cottonwood trees.

BRIGHT ANGEL CAMPGROUND

This charming campground, located at the bottom of the Canyon near Phantom Ranch, is accessible via the Bright Angel Trail or the South Kaibab Trail. The campground is situated above the banks of Bright Angel Creek, and each of the 32 campsites comes with a picnic table and fire ring. If you don't want to lug your gear up or down the Canyon, arrange for a mule to carry up to 30 pounds of gear for $60 one-way. Call 888-297-2757 for more information about "Duffel Service."

GETTING AROUND THE SOUTH RIM

BY CAR

Exploring the South Rim in your own car lets you hop from sight to sight at your own pace, but traffic and parking can be a pain during the busy summer months. Furthermore, Hermit Road and the road to Yaki Point are closed to private vehicle traffic from March 1 through November 30. No matter what time of year you visit, it's generally best to park your car at one of Grand Canyon Village's five parking areas and use the park's free shuttle system. You'll still need a car to explore Desert View Drive, which is not serviced by free shuttles, although a narrated 4-hour tour is offered (see Bus Tours, following page).

BY SHUTTLE

The park runs several free shuttle buses that make frequent stops in Grand Canyon Village and along Hermit Drive. Exact schedules vary from season to season, so pick up a copy of the park's free newspaper, *The Guide*, for current schedules and other information. The most popular shuttle routes are the **Village Route**, which loops through parking areas, viewpoints, and lodges in Grand Canyon Village, and the **Hermits Rest Route**, which runs back and forth along Hermit Drive. Two additional shuttles provide access to the South Kaibab Trail trailhead at Yaki Point: the **Kaibab Trail Route** runs between the Canyon View Information Plaza and Yaki Point, and the **Hiker's Express Route** shuttles early morning hikers from Bright Angel Lodge and the Backcountry Information Center to Yaki Point.

ON FOOT

One of the best ways to explore the South Rim is to walk along the **Rim Trail**, which stretches from Pipe Creek Vista, about half a mile south of Mather Point, to Hermits Rest. From end to end the Rim Trail is 13 miles long, but you can pick it up at any viewpoint. Many visitors enjoy hiking to viewpoints along Hermit Road, then riding the free shuttle back to Grand Canyon Village. Check the shuttle schedule before you go; not every viewpoint along Hermit Road is serviced by the shuttle.

BY BICYCLE

Bicycles are allowed on all paved and unpaved roads on the South Rim, but they're prohibited from all other trails (including the Rim Trail). If passing cars don't bother you, bicycles are one of the best ways to explore the South Rim. But bicyclists must obey all traffic regulations. And when riding on narrow Hermit Road, bicyclists should pull to the right shoulder of the road and dismount when large vehicles are attempting to pass.

DINING

Almost all South Rim restaurants are located in Grand Canyon Village (the lone exception is the small cafeteria at Desert View). During the busy summer months, restaurants that don't accept reservations fill up fast, and waiting times can sometimes exceed two hours. If you want to beat the crowds, arrive before sunset.

ARIZONA ROOM

This popular dinner spot, located in Bright Angel Lodge, serves standard American food. Open 4:30 p.m.–10 p.m. No reservations.

BRIGHT ANGEL RESTAURANT

Serves breakfast, lunch and dinner in Bright Angel Lodge. Open 6:30 a.m.–10 p.m. No reservations.

EL TOVAR

The finest, and most expensive dining on the South Rim. Prices top $20 an entree, but the soft lighting, dark wood paneling, and elegant atmosphere are definitely worth it. Reservations, often made days in advance, are only available for dinner. Open for breakfast, lunch, and dinner (928-638-2526 x6432).

MASWIK CAFETERIA

Cafeteria-style food with Mexican and Italian selections. Located in Maswik Lodge. Open 6 a.m.–10 p.m.

YAVAPAI CAFETERIA

Cafeteria-style fast food. Open 7 a.m.–8 p.m. (6 a.m.–9 p.m. in the summer).

ENTERTAINMENT

RANGER PROGRAMS

Free ranger programs are offered throughout the year. Topics include history, geology, wildlife, and more. Check *The Guide* for seasonal times and locations.

BUS TOURS

Xanterra (the company that runs the park's lodges) offers narrated bus tours along the South Rim. The **Desert View Tour** (4 hours, $30) travels along Desert View Drive. The **Hermit Road Tour** (2 hours, $20) travels along Hermit Drive. Sunrise and sunset tours ($15) also run May–October, and a package deal offering two tours is available for $40. Children under 16 ride for free. For more information contact the transportation desk at any lodge.

MULE TRIPS

Day and overnight mule trips depart daily from the South Rim. **Day trips** (7 hours, $145 per person) descend 3,500 feet down the Bright Angel Trail to Plateau Point, then return via the same route. **Overnight trips** follow the Bright Angel Trail to the bottom, where riders spend the night at Phantom Ranch, then return the next day via the South Kaibab Trail; Cost: $370 for one person, $660 for two people. Rides offering an extra night at Phantom Ranch are also available. Reservations should be made as far in advance as possible (they're accepted up to one year in advance). Contact Xanterra for additional information (888-297-2757, www.grandcanyonlodges.com).

ART EXHIBITS

Kolb Studio (p.136) showcases constantly changing art exhibits. Check The Guide for information about the current exhibit.

GRAND CANYON MUSIC FESTIVAL

Weekend and mid-week concerts are offered every September at the Shrine of the Ages. Tickets: $25 adults, $8 children (www.grandcanyonmusicfest.org).

SERVICES

CANYON VILLAGE MARKETPLACE

This general store in Market Plaza (next to Yavapai Lodge) sells groceries, film, camping gear, outdoor supplies, and a wide selection of other items.

GAS

There are no gas stations in Grand Canyon Village. The closest gas stations are in the town of Tusayan and at Desert View.

POST OFFICE

Located in Market Plaza. Open every weekday and half-day Saturday.

COIN-OPERATED SHOWERS & LAUNDROMAT

Located near the entrance to Mather Campground.

PET KENNEL

Offers lodging for pets (which aren't allowed in park lodges or on inner canyon trails). Reservations are recommended (928-638-0534).

GRAND CANYON GARAGE

Offers auto repair, emergency 24-hour service, and towing (928-638-2631).

Tusayan
BASICS

TUSAYAN IS A tiny town located a few miles south of Grand Canyon Village. Sandwiched between Grand Canyon National Park to the north and the Kaibab National Forest to the south, it's the only private property anywhere near the South Rim's most popular sights. As such, Tusayan revolves entirely around Grand Canyon tourism. The town consists of a short stretch of hotels, fast food restaurants, and shops lining either side of AZ-64. Just south of the main drag is tiny Grand Canyon Airport, which offers popular sightseeing flights (p.31).

LODGING

Surprisingly, lodging in Tusayan is often more expensive than lodging in the park. The reason: many of Tusayan's hotels offer modern luxuries such as swimming pools, spas, and other amenities unavailable at park hotels. Room rates during peak tourist season range anywhere from $100 to $200 per night; winter rates are generally lower.

BEST WESTERN GRAND CANYON SQUIRE INN
Offers large rooms, an outdoor pool, tennis courts, spa, sports bar, three restaurants, and a bowling alley (800-622-6966, www.grandcanyonsquire.com).

GRAND CANYON QUALITY INN
Standard Quality Inn with an outdoor pool and indoor hot tub. (800-221-2222, www.grandcanyonqualityinn.com)

THE GRAND HOTEL
This dramatic hotel, styled like a grand rustic lodge, offers an indoor pool, restaurant and live entertainment. (888-634-7263, www.visitgrandcanyon.com)

SEVEN MILE LODGE
This is by far the cheapest option in Tusayan, but they do not take reservations. Rooms are available first come, first served. (928-638-2291)

For lodging links and additional lodging options in Flagstaff and Williams, visit www.jameskaiser.com

HOLIDAY INN EXPRESS
Standard Holiday Inn with an indoor pool and spa. Also offers Kids Suites with bunk beds, TV, VCR and video games. (888-473-2269, www.gcanyon.com/hi)

RODEWAY INN RED FEATHER LODGE
Budget motel with outdoor pool, hot tub, and fitness center. (800-538-2345, www.redfeatherlodge.com)

CAMPING

GRAND CANYON CAMPER VILLAGE
Offers tent sites ($25) and RV sites ($50, full hook-up). Coin-operated showers nearby. Reservations only available for RV sites with hook-ups (928-638-2887).

TEN X CAMPGROUND
Operated by the Kaibab National Forest, two miles south of Tusayan. Open May–September, Cost: $10 per vehicle (928-638-2443).

DINING

CAFE TUSAYAN
Standard American food. Located next to the Red Feather Lodge. (928-638-2151)

CANYON STAR
American and southwestern food. Located in the Grand Hotel (928-638-3333).

CORONADO ROOM
American and southwestern food. Open only for dinner. Located in the Best Western Grand Canyon Squire (928-638-2681).

YIPPEI-EI-O! STEAKHOUSE
Classic steakhouse. Open for lunch (summer only) and dinner (928-638-2780).

WE COOK PIZZA AND PASTA
Serves, you guessed it, pizza and pasta. Open lunch and dinner (928-638-2278).

ENTERTAINMENT

IMAX THEATER
Year after year, the IMAX film *Grand Canyon—The Hidden Secrets* lures hordes of visitors to its 70-foot screen. The 35-minute movie plays every hour on the half hour. Cost: $10 adults, $7 children under 12.

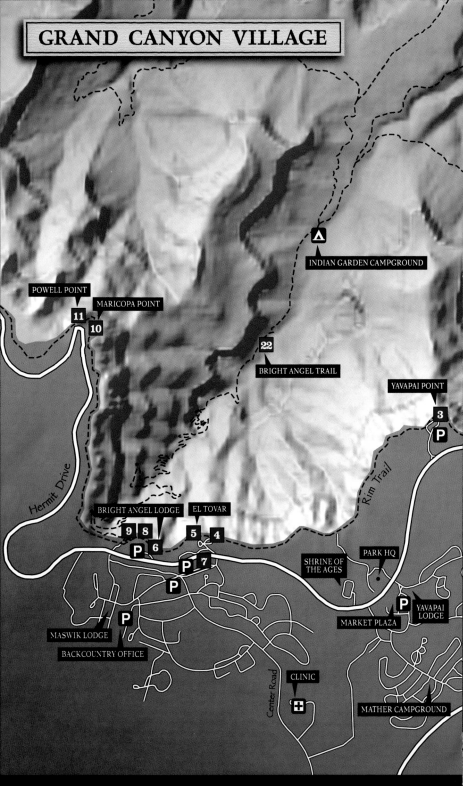

GRAND CANYON VILLAGE

INDIAN GARDEN CAMPGROUND

POWELL POINT

MARICOPA POINT

11

10

22

BRIGHT ANGEL TRAIL

YAVAPAI POINT

3

P

Hermit Drive

Rim Trail

BRIGHT ANGEL LODGE

EL TOVAR

9 8

P 6

5 4

P 7

P

PARK HQ

SHRINE OF
THE AGES

P

YAVAPAI
LODGE

P

MASWIK LODGE

BACKCOUNTRY OFFICE

MARKET PLAZA

Center Road

CLINIC

MATHER CAMPGROUND

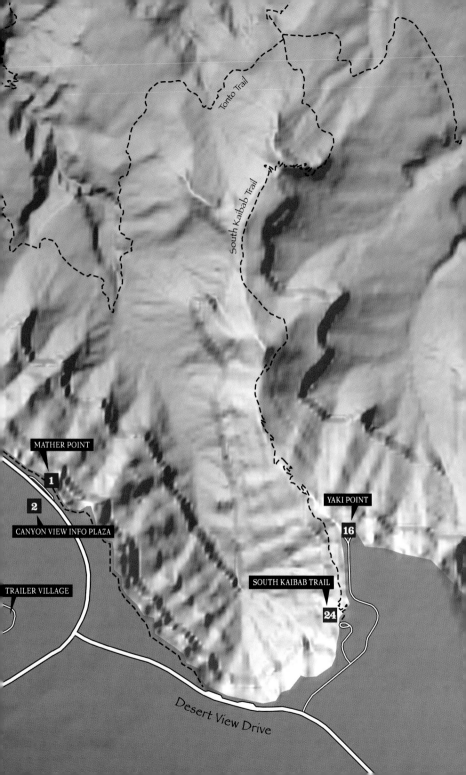

MATHER POINT

1

2

CANYON VIEW INFO PLAZA

TRAILER VILLAGE

Tonto Trail

South Kaibab Trail

YAKI POINT

16

SOUTH KAIBAB TRAIL

24

Desert View Drive

1 Mather Point

Mather Point is the most popular viewpoint in the park—but it's popularity is mostly due to its close proximity to the park entrance. Still, the views are fantastic. Although the scenery stretches on for miles, only about one third of the total length of the Grand Canyon is visible. Look to the east and you'll see pointy Vishnu Temple rising to a height of 7,533 feet in the Inner Canyon. Vishnu Temple was named by the early geologist Clarence Dutton, who felt it bore "a surprising resemblance to an Oriental pagoda."

Mather Point is named for Stephen Mather, the first director of the National Park Service. In 1914 Mather, a wealthy industrialist who made his fortune mining borax in Death Valley, complained to Interior Secretary Franklin Lane about the management of America's national parks. Lane's response: "If you don't like the way the national parks are being run, come on down to Washington and run them yourself." Mather did just that. He joined the National Park Service in 1916 and spent the next 13 years of his life shaping a strong vision for America's national parks.

Although the views from Mather Point are stunning, its popularity makes it one of the most congested spots in the park, *especially* in the summer. Savvy visitors realize there are equally fantastic viewpoints nearby, such as Yaki Point (p.158) to the east and Hopi Point (p.146) to the west. If the crowds at Mather Point are overwhelming, don't hesitate to move on. You can always come back later.

Note: Parking is limited to 60 minutes at Mather Point.

2 Canyon View Info Plaza

This cluster of buildings, nestled in the woods across from Mather Point, serves as the park's main welcoming center. On the right is the visitor center, which features a ranger-staffed help desk and several exhibits about the park. Across the way is Books & More, a store operated by the non-profit Grand Canyon Association that sells books, maps, postcards, and more. Restrooms are also located nearby.

Canyon View Information Plaza, which opened in 2000, was originally intended as the terminus of a light rail system that would shuttle visitors into the park from large parking lots in Tusayan. Visitors could leave their cars in Tusayan, hop the train to Canyon View Information Plaza, and then explore the South Rim using the park's free shuttle system. (The open air exhibits were built to give visitors something to look at while they waited for the train.) Unfortunately, budgetary issues have delayed construction of the light rail.

Note: There's no parking at Canyon View Information Plaza. The closest parking is at Mather Point. If the parking area at Mather Point is full, you can park in Grand Canyon Village and hop a free shuttle back to Canyon View Information Plaza or follow the new Greenway Trail, a walking and biking trail that links Grand Canyon Village with Canyon View Information Plaza.

3 Yavapai Point

Yavapai Observation Center, perched on the edge of Yavapai Point, is an historic building that served as the South Rim's first museum and interpretive center. Originally built in 1928, it has large viewing windows that provide sweeping panoramas of the Canyon, making it a great place to take shelter in bad weather. Inside there are exhibits and a small store selling books and postcards. Restrooms are located in a building next to the parking area.

One of the most prominent sights from Yavapai Point is Bright Angel Canyon, which slices eight miles into the North Rim. The North Kaibab Trail (p.272) runs through much of Bright Angel Canyon. As the trail nears the Colorado River, it passes by Phantom Ranch, a collection of small buildings offering the only overnight lodging at the bottom of Grand Canyon. Phantom Ranch is visible from Yavapai Point—look for the faint patch of green foliage running east-west at the head of Bright Angel Canyon.

Another famous feature visible from Yavapai Point is the broad, flat Tonto Platform, located just above the dark Inner Gorge near the bottom of the Canyon. Eagle-eyed visitors can spot the faint Tonto Trail running east-west along the Tonto Platform south of the Colorado River.

Yavapai is a Paiute Indian word that means "Sun People." The word refers to a group of Indians who once lived in central and western Arizona.

4 Hopi House

This unique building was designed by Mary Colter, a famous architect who designed many of the park's historic buildings. Hopi House was Colter's first assignment for the Grand Canyon. It was patterned after buildings at Old Oraibi, a Hopi Village 80 miles east of Grand Canyon which is the oldest continuously inhabited town in America. Hopi Indians helped in its construction, and the stone exterior, corner fireplaces, and thatched ceilings are all characteristic of Hopi design. When the building opened in 1905, Hopi craftsmen lived on its upper floors and nightly Hopi dances were often held out front. Today crafts from several Southwestern tribes are sold inside.

MARY COLTER

In the early 1900s, a time when few women practiced architecture, Mary Colter was hard at work designing some of the most spectacular buildings in the Southwest. Many of her creations are found at Grand Canyon, and many are now listed as historic landmarks. Among her Grand Canyon creations: Lookout Studio, Hermits Rest, Desert View Watchtower, and Phantom Ranch.

Hopi Dancers

5 El Tovar Hotel

The historic hotel, designed by architect Charles Whittlesey, offers the finest lodging in Grand Canyon. Over the years El Tovar has played host to such 20th century icons as Theodore Roosevelt, Albert Einstein, and Paul McCartney. Today the hotel continues to offer the finest lodging and dining in the park. Even if you're not a guest, El Tovar's dramatic front lobby is worth a quick look, and its bar and restaurant are open to the public.

When El Tovar first opened in 1905, it was one of the most technologically advanced hotels in the Southwest. Among its high-tech amenities: electric lights, steam heat, hot and cold water, and indoor plumbing—a stark contrast to the primitive rooms, cheap beds, and outhouses that had previously defined luxury at Grand Canyon. For many years fresh fruits and vegetables were grown in El Tovar's greenhouses, and local farm animals provided fresh eggs and milk.

El Tovar was named after Don Pedro de Tovar, a lieutenant of Spanish explorer Francisco Vásquez de Coronado, who led the first Spanish expedition through the Southwest in 1540. Ironically, Don Pedro de Tovar never set eyes on Grand Canyon. Coronado sent another of his men, García Lopez de Cárdenas, to explore Grand Canyon. But when the Fred Harvey Company built the hotel, they already had a Cardenas Hotel in Colorado, so they chose the name El Tovar.

6 Bright Angel Lodge

Even if you're not a guest at this historic hotel, Bright Angel Lodge is worth a quick glimpse if you're hiking along the Rim Trail. Inside you'll find a restaurant, a bar, and a gift shop. There's also a small museum with historic photos and a fireplace built out of actual Grand Canyon rocks—arranged floor to ceiling in their proper geological sequence. A small booth to the left of the front desk also offers information on ranger programs, bus tours, mule rides, and other daily South Rim activities.

When Bright Angel Lodge first opened in 1896, it consisted of nothing more than a collection of primitive tents. Guests walked from tent to tent along an elevated boardwalk that protected them from horse droppings (a prominent feature of Grand Canyon Village back then). Over the years, the lodge expanded to include a log cabin with eight guest rooms. Cabin rooms were rented for $2.50 per night, and tents were rented for $1.50. Later the lodge expanded, and the current buildings were built in the 1930s.

View near Bright Angel Lodge

7 | Santa Fe Train Depot

This rustic train station, located just south of El Tovar Hotel, is the only train station in any U.S. national park. It also claims to be the last surviving train station in America built entirely out of logs.

Train service first arrived at the South Rim in 1901, following the completion of a spur line connecting the South Rim to the town of Williams (60 miles to the south). Before the spur line was completed, the most dependable form of transportation to the South Rim was a bumpy, all-day stagecoach ride that coast $20. When the spur line was completed, visitors could travel to the South Rim in four hours for $3.50. Not surprisingly, the railroad brought a flood of new visitors to Grand Canyon. Within a few decades, however, most people were arriving by car, and in 1968 falling ridership forced the railroad to shut down. The last departing train carried only three passengers. Then, in 1989, the railroad roared back to life. With traffic and congestion increasing in the park, a new generation of riders rediscovered the railroad's convenience and charm. Today, trains depart daily from Williams.

8 Lookout Studio

This small stone building, perched on the edge of the Canyon just west of Bright Angel Lodge, offers stunning views and a small gift shop inside. Lookout Studio was designed by Mary Colter, who wanted the building to blend seamlessly into the landscape. This followed the design principles set forth by landscape architect Frederick Law Olmstead, who believed that, whenever possible, buildings in national parks should reflect the architecture of indigenous cultures. The indigenous cultures of the Southwest built some of the most impressive structures in America, and Colter incorporated many of their architectural techniques—stone walls, flat roofs, timber supports—into her design. After it was built, Lookout Studio became famous for its sweeping views. An old Santa Fe Railroad brochure once boasted that visitors who peered through the telescopes installed at Lookout Studio could, "traverse the Canyon trails, explore the rugged portions of the interior, or see its faraway reaches."

Lookout Studio, 1915

9 Kolb Studio

Today Kolb Studio houses a well-stocked bookstore and art gallery with changing exhibits. But for over 70 years it was the home of Emery Kolb, one of Grand Canyon's earliest and most famous photographers. Emery and his brother Ellsworth came to Grand Canyon in 1902. Shortly after their arrival, they set up a photography studio on the rim and started hawking souvenir photos of mule riders descending the nearby Bright Angel Trail. But as Saturday Evening Post writer Irvin S. Cobb wrote of one such mule ride, "Just under the first terrace a halt is made while the official photographer takes a picture; and when you get back he has your finished copy ready for you, so you can see for yourself just how pale and haggard and wall-eyed and how much like a typhoid patient you looked."

Tourist photos paid the bills, but the Kolb brothers' passion was exploring Grand Canyon and capturing their daredevil exploits on film. In 1911 the brothers ran the Colorado River from Wyoming to California—the first time anyone had accomplished the feat since John Wesley Powell in 1869. But the Kolbs' journey wasn't just for the record books. The brothers filmed their journey and made the first-ever movie of a river trip through Grand Canyon. The Kolbs screened their movie at lectures across the country, and it played continuously at Kolb Studio until Emery's death in 1976.

Emery Kolb

The Kolb brothers

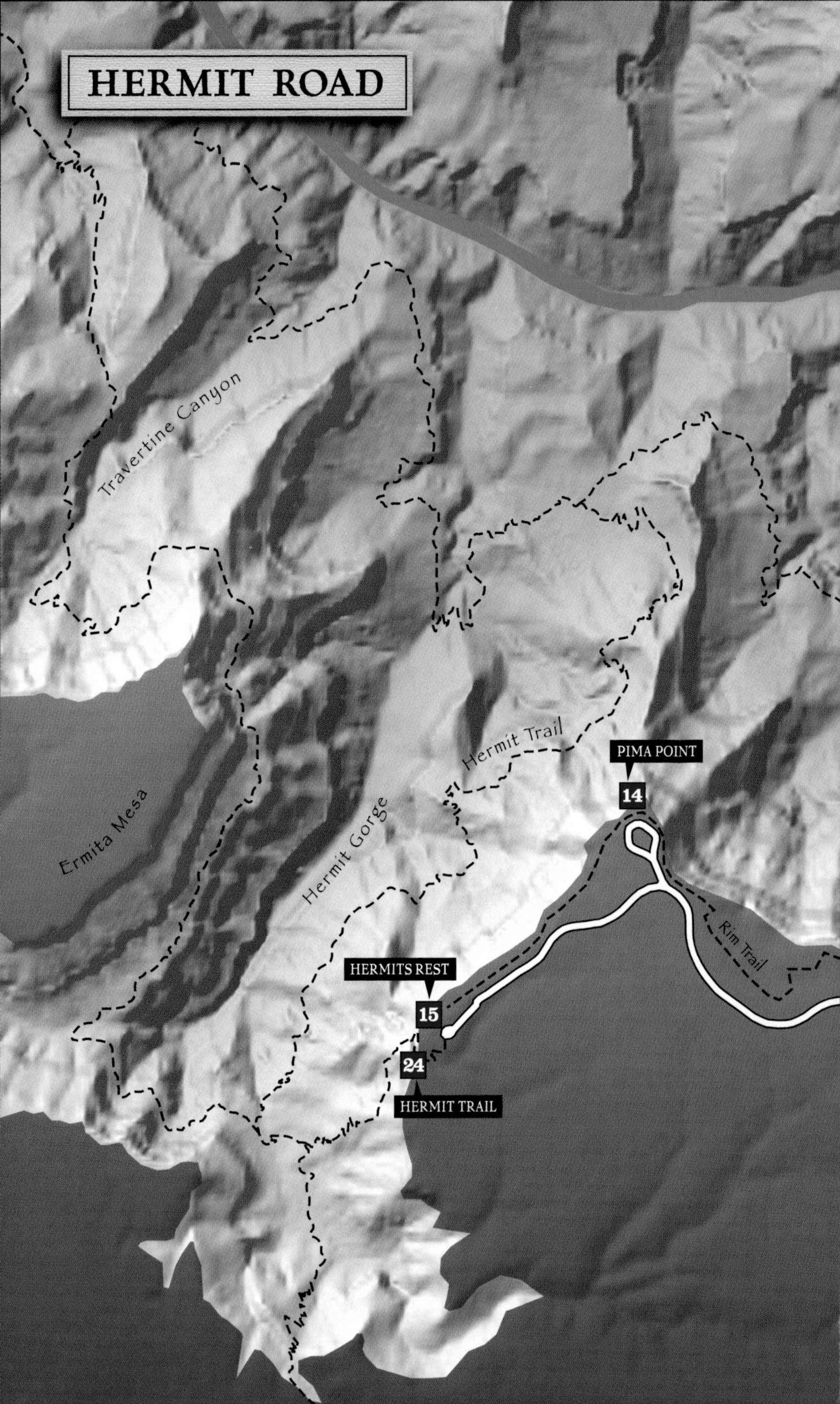

HERMIT ROAD

Travertine Canyon

Ermita Mesa

Hermit Gorge

Hermit Trail

PIMA POINT

14

HERMITS REST

15

24

HERMIT TRAIL

Rim Trail

10 Maricopa Point

Maricopa Point offers Hermit Road's first sweeping views of western Grand Canyon. Just west of the point are the decaying remains of the Lost Orphan Mine—one of the most productive uranium mines in America in the 1950s. Prior to the 1950s, the mine site was home to a 20-cabin resort owned by Will Rogers, Jr.

IMAGINE, IF YOU can, a monster of a hollow hundreds of miles long and a mile deep, and anywhere from ten to sixteen miles wide, with a mountain range—the most wonderful mountain range in the world—planted in it ... Imagine all this spread out beneath the unflawed turquoise of the Arizona sky and washed in the liquid gold of the Arizona sunshine—and if you imagine hard enough and keep it up long enough you may begin, in the course of eight or ten years, to have a faint, a very faint and shadowy conception of this spot where the shamed scheme of creation is turned upside down and the very womb of the world is laid bare before our imperious eyes. Then go to Arizona and see it all for yourself, and you will realize what an entirely inadequate and deficient thing the human imagination is.

—Irvin S. Cobb, 1913

11 Powell Point

Powell Point is named for John Wesley Powell, the famous explorer who led the first Colorado River expedition through Grand Canyon in 1869. In 1920 a monument to Powell was built and dedicated here. The ceremony was attended by Powell's niece and grand-niece, and the monument was christened by the Secretary of the Interior with water from the Colorado River.

Powell's Grand Canyon adventure has often been called the last great expedition of the American West. Prior to the trip, no one knew what existed along much of the Colorado River. There were rumors of giant waterfalls at the bottom of Grand Canyon and places where the river disappeared underground. Accepting these risks, Powell, a one-armed Civil War veteran, and nine other men—none with any whitewater experience—launched four boats from Green River, Wyoming, in May 1869. Three months later, two boats carrying six skeletal men emerged from Grand Canyon near present-day Lake Mead. Four men had abandoned the grueling journey along the way, three of whom died trying to reach civilization. The names of those four men do not appear on the monument. See page 81 for more on Powell's extraordinary journey.

12 Hopi Point

Named in honor of the Hopi Indians, Hopi Point offers some of Hermit Road's most sweeping views. Because it juts out farther into the Canyon than any other accessible viewpoint on the South Rim, Hopi Point is one of Grand Canyon's most popular sunset destinations. It also offers terrific views of several stone "temples" rising from the depths of the Canyon. Almost directly ahead lies flat-topped Shiva Temple (named for the Hindu destroyer), and just east of Shiva is pointy Isis Temple (named for the Egyptian goddess of nature). Cheops Pyramid (named for the Great Pyramid of Cheops) lies below Isis to the east. To the north-east, Hopi Point offers terrific views of Zoroaster Temple (see following page).

AT LENGTH, AS THE sun draws near the horizon, the great drama of the day begins ... Slowly the myriad of details have come out and the walls are flecked with lines of minute tracery ... Stronger and sharper becomes the relief of each projection ... A thousand forms, hitherto unseen or obscure, start up within the abyss, and stand forth in strength and animation. All things seem to grow in beauty, power, and dimensions. What was grand before has become majestic, the majestic becomes sublime, and, ever expanding and developing, the sublime passes beyond the reach of our faculties and becomes transcendent.

—Clarence Dutton, 1882

ZOROASTER TEMPLE

Zoroaster Temple, which lies just east of Bright Angel Canyon, is one of Grand Canyon's most graceful rock formations. Topping out at 7,128 feet, it towers over 4,500 feet above the Colorado River. The temple is named after Zoroaster, a Persian prophet who founded Zoroastrianism several centuries before Christ. As one of the most prominent landmarks in the park, Zoroaster Temple has lured many rugged climbers over the years. The first ascent of "Zoro" was made on September 23, 1958, by David Ganci and Rick Tidrick, who spent four days trekking to the top from Phantom Ranch.

13 Mohave Point

Mohave Point is named in honor of the Mojave Indians, who once lived along the lower Colorado River south of Grand Canyon. (And that's not a typo you just saw—as a general rule, "Mojave" is spelled with a "j" for locations in California and with an "h" for locations in Arizona.) The long, rocky promontory that stretches down from Mohave Point is called the Alligator. Hermit Rapid, on the Colorado River, is also visible from Mohave Point. The rapid, like many rapids in Grand Canyon, formed when debris washed into the river from an adjacent side canyon.

I MAGINE, WAY DOWN there at the bottom, a stream visible only at certain favored points because of the mighty intervening ribs and chines of rock—a stream that appears to you as a torpidly crawling yellow worm, its wrinkling back spangled with tarnished white specks, but which is really a wide, deep, brawling, rushing river—the Colorado—full of torrents and rapids; and those white specks you see are the tops of enormous rocks in its bed.

—Irvin S. Cobb, 1913

14 Pima Point

Pima Point, named after the Pima Indians of southern Arizona, offers one of the best views of the Colorado River along the South Rim. Although the Pima Indians refer to themselves as *Akimel O'odham* ("River People"), the name Pima is derived from *pim'ach*, which means "I don't understand you." This was probably the unfortunate response given to early Spanish explorers when they asked the *Akimel O'odham* what they called themselves.

In 1912 the Fred Harvey Company built Hermit Camp, an upscale cluster of tent cabins, 3,600 feet below Pima Point. Hermit Camp was located along the Hermit Trail—the Santa Fe Railroad's free alternative to the Bright Angel Trail, which was then operated as a private toll road. Hermit Camp boasted such amenities as showers, telephones, a dining hall, a stable, and a blacksmith's shop. Guests often stayed for several days, spending their time exploring the rugged surroundings on foot or horseback.

In 1926 a 6,300-foot aerial tram was built connecting Pima Point and Hermit Camp. At the time it was the longest single-span tram in the United States. The tram ride was about a half hour each way, but the modern marvel did not last long. In the late 1920s the park service gained control of the Bright Angel Trail, which was located closer to popular hotels on the rim, and lifted its toll. Before long, most Grand Canyon visitors were descending the Canyon via the Bright Angel Trail and spending the night at Phantom Ranch. In 1930 Hermit Camp shut down for good. Its remains were burned and the tram was removed.

Hermit Camp

15 Hermits Rest

Hermits Rest marks the end of Hermit Road. Its main attraction is a whimsical stone building with a giant fireplace. Drinks, snacks, and gifts are available inside, and restrooms are located nearby. Hermits Rest was built by the Santa Fe Railroad in 1914. Like many famous buildings in the park, it was designed by architect Mary Colter, who wanted to create a building that looked like the kind of place where a hermit might live. In addition to the main building, she also designed a limestone arch with an authentic New Mexico mission bell.

The "hermit" of Hermits Rest was an early prospector named Louis Boucher, who lived by himself in the canyon below. Although labeled a hermit, Boucher was, by all accounts, a friendly man who simply liked living alone. Originally from Quebec, Boucher arrived at Grand Canyon around 1891. Like many prospectors, he had several horses and mules. Unlike many prospectors, he also kept goldfish in a small trough. Boucher also planted an orchard that provided him with peaches, oranges and figs. After spending two decades searching in vain for a rich mineral strike, Boucher moved to Utah in 1909.

Louis Boucher

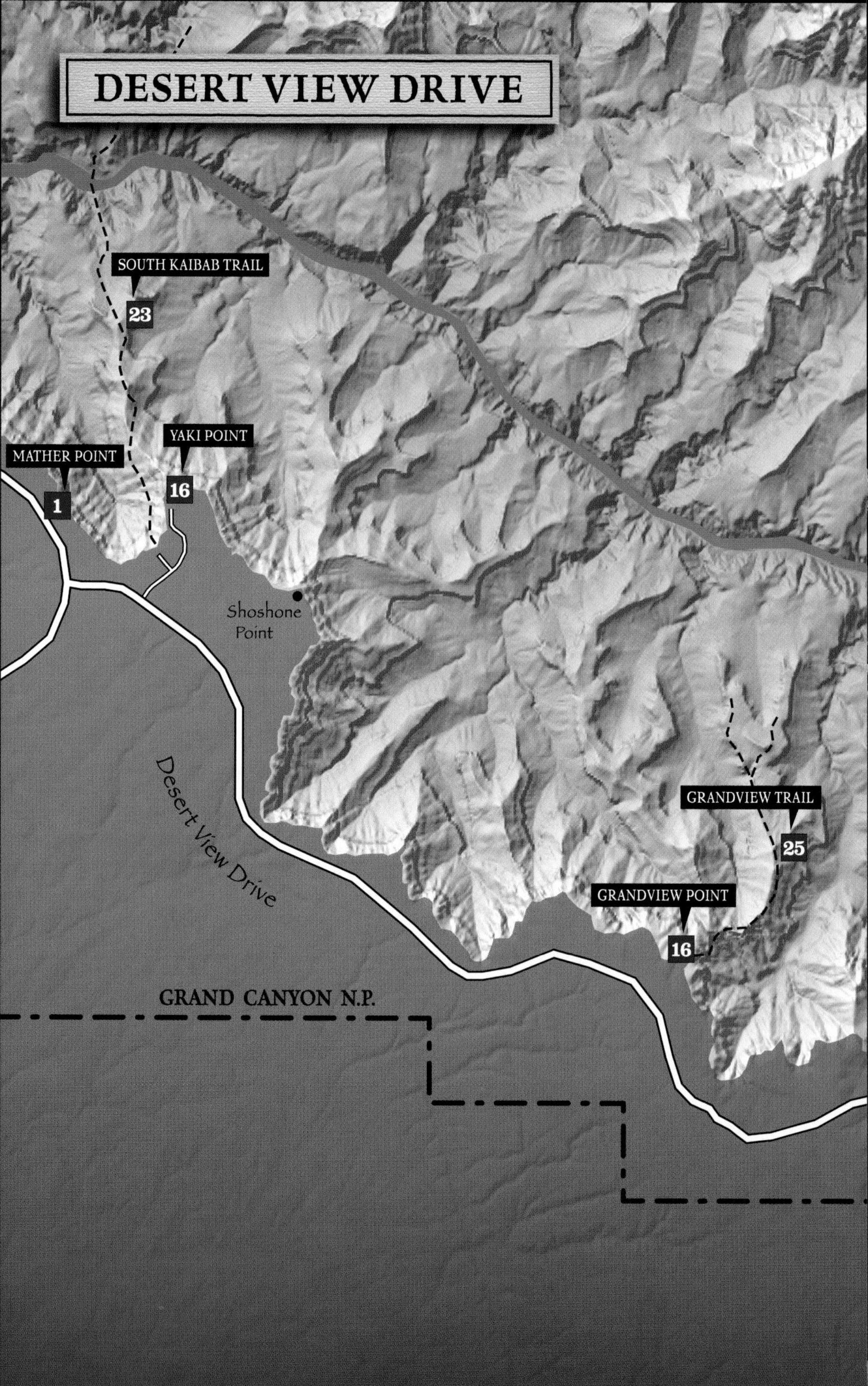

DESERT VIEW DRIVE

SOUTH KAIBAB TRAIL

23

YAKI POINT

16

MATHER POINT

1

Shoshone
Point

Desert View Drive

GRANDVIEW TRAIL

25

GRANDVIEW POINT

16

GRAND CANYON N.P.

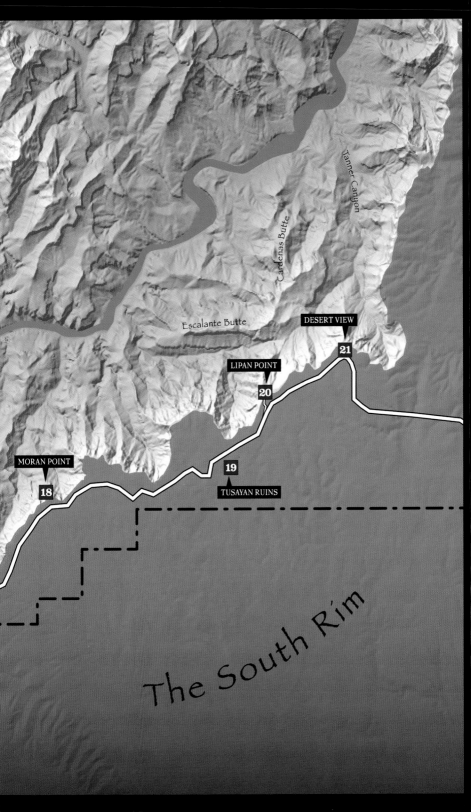

Tanner Canyon

Cardenas Butte

Escalante Butte

DESERT VIEW

21

LIPAN POINT

20

MORAN POINT

18

19

TUSAYAN RUINS

The South Rim

16 Yaki Point

Stretching far into the Canyon, Yaki Point provides sweeping views to the east and west, making it one of the best sunrise spots on the South Rim. The road to Yaki Point is only accessible via the park's free shuttle (check *The Guide* for shuttle schedules). The South Kaibab Trail (p.180), which offers the South Rim's most direct route to the bottom of the Canyon, starts just south of Yaki Point—you can see the trail as it cuts diagonally across the east face of O'Neil Butte. Yaki Point was supposedly named by George Wharton James in honor of Mexico's Yaqui Indians, who were victims of mass genocide in the early 1900s.

> IMAGINE—IF IT BE WINTER—snowdrifts above, with desert flowers blooming alongside the drifts, and down below great stretches of green verdure; imagine two or three separate snow-storms visibly raging at different points, with clear, bright stretches of distance intervening between them, and nearer maybe a splendid rainbow arching downward into the great void; for these meteorological three-ring circuses are not uncommon at certain seasons.
>
> —Irvin S. Cobb, 1913

Vishnu Temple

17 Grandview Point

At 7,406 feet, Grandview Point is one of the highest points on the South Rim. In addition to grand views, Grandview Point is notable for its many ponderosa pines, which grow only at high elevations. Grandview Point is also the jumping off point for the popular Grandview Trail (p.192).

Before the railroad arrived at Grand Canyon Village in 1901, Grandview Point was the hub of all tourist activity in the park. In 1886 John Hance, a prospector turned tour guide, built the first hotel here. Within a few years another prospector named Pete Berry had also built the Grandview Hotel (above). But after the railroad arrived in Grand Canyon Village, few tourists were willing to make the additional trek to Grandview Point. By 1908 both hotels had shut down. A few years later, Berry sold his landholdings to newspaper tycoon William Randolph Hearst, who tore down the Grandview Hotel in 1929. Hearst planned to build his own hotel on the property, but a federal court forced him to sell his land to the park in 1939.

During its short-lived hotel era, Grandview Point was also a popular jumping off point for miners seeking mineral riches below the rim. In 1890 Pete Berry, Ralph Cameron, and Niles Cameron established the Last Chance copper mine at Horseshoe Mesa, just below Grandview Point. The mine contained an extremely high-grade ore (up to 70 percent copper), but when copper prices crashed in 1907, mining operations at Last Chance shut down.

Moran Point

18 Moran Point

This impressive overlook is named after Thomas Moran, one of America's most famous and influential landscape painters. Although born in England in 1837, Moran moved to America with his family in the mid-1800s—a time when landscape painting exhibitions drew blockbuster crowds in large cities. In the days before color photography, monumental landscape paintings offered the public a rare glimpse of America's wild and exotic places. Inspired by these works, young Thomas Moran decided to become a landscape painter. His dramatic paintings of Yellowstone were critical in the establishment of Yellowstone National Park in 1872. The following year, Moran joined legendary explorer John Wesley Powell on an expedition to Grand Canyon. He later wrote of his experience, "it was by far the most awfully grand and impressive scene that I have ever yet seen." Moran later returned with geologist Clarence Dutton, and his works from both of these trips were published in best-selling books. One of his paintings, *The Grand Chasm of the Colorado*, hung in the U.S. Capitol for many years. Deeply moved by his Grand Canyon experiences, Moran returned to the Canyon every winter for over 20 years.

19 Tusayan Ruin

These ruins mark the location of Tusayan, a small Ancestral Puebloan village that existed here 800 years ago. The remains were partially excavated in 1930, and today they are the most visited archaeological site in Arizona (a distinction that has more to do with its high-traffic Grand Canyon location than the ruins themselves, which are a bit underwhelming). A 0.1-mile path guides visitors through the ruins, and free ranger tours are offered that help bring Tusayan to life. A small museum is also located near the parking area.

At its peak, Tusayan was probably home to no more than 30 people, and archaeologists believe that it was only occupied for about 20 years. Tusayan was one of the last Ancestral Puebloan sites occupied in Grand Canyon, constructed shortly before the collapse of Ancestral Puebloan society around A.D. 1200. The most prominent feature of the village was a large, 14-room building with two *kivas* (ceremonial rooms) located nearby. Crops such as beans, corn and squash were grown in a field to the east, but because there is no permanent source of water within seven miles of Tusayan, stone walls were built in the fields to retain runoff. Despite this access to fresh food, evidence indicates that health problems were common among Ancestral Puebloans. Chimneys and windows were largely absent from their structures, and smoke-filled rooms contributed to respiratory difficulties. Skeletal remains also reveal teeth worn down to the dentine, the result of eating stone-ground cornmeal.

20 Lipan Point

Lipan Point offers one of the most sweeping views on the South Rim. It's also one of the best places to see rocks of the Grand Canyon Supergroup, which are tilted at a 20-degree angle and range in age from 800 million to 1.2 billion years old. Although absent from much of the Canyon, the Grand Canyon Supergroup is easily visible above the sharp bend in the Colorado River across from Lipan Point. Nearby Cardenas Butte was named in honor of García Lopez de Cárdenas, who led a group of Spanish explorers to a spot near Lipan Point in 1540.

IMAGINE THESE MOUNTAIN peaks—hundreds upon hundreds of them—rising one behind the other, stretching away in endless, serried rank... imagine them splashed and splattered over with all the earthly colors you ever saw and a lot of unearthly colors you never saw before; imagine them carved and fretted and scrolled into all shapes—tabernacles, pyramids, battleships, obelisks, Moorish palaces—the Moorish suggestion is especially pronounced both in coloring and in shapes—mountains, minarets, temples, turrets, castles, spires, domes, tents, tepees, wigwams, shafts.

—Irvin S. Cobb, 1913

21 Desert View

Desert View is the final stop on Desert View Drive. At 7,438 feet, it's also one of the highest points on the South Rim. In addition to panoramic views, Desert View is notable for Desert View Watchtower, designed by Mary Colter and built in 1932. Colter based Desert View Watchtower on towers found at ancient pueblos in the Four Corners region. A circular staircase leads to the top of the 70-foot tower, which is decorated with reproductions of Ancestral Puebloan petroglyphs and depictions of Hopi legends.

DAYS AND WEEKS can be given to Desert View without exhausting the scene or the interest. You are away from the hotel and the crowd, and can see things like a lone eagle from your point of rock ... the Canyon here is happily disposed for morning and evening effects because it runs practically east and west, and the light strikes not so much across it as along its length ... One by one the tops of the buttes and points and promontories take up and carry on the light far down the Canyon. First one glows and shifts into a bright garb, and then another farther on repeats the litany of color.

—John C. Van Dyke, 1920

⚔ BRIGHT ANGEL TRAIL ⚔

SUMMARY   The Bright Angel Trail is the most popular trail on the South Rim—and with good reason. Starting near several popular hotels, it provides convenient access below the rim, offering dramatic views of the Inner Canyon. Although steep and challenging, it's well-maintained and makes a terrific introduction to Canyon hiking. Day hikers should consider 1.5 Mile Resthouse (2–4 hours, round trip) or 3 Mile Resthouse (4–6 hours, round trip). Both offer clean drinking water from May through September. Halfway down the trail is Indian Garden Campground, and a nearby spur trail heads 1.5 miles to Plateau Point, one of the finest Inner Canyon viewpoints in the park. Past Indian Garden the Bright Angel Trail continues its steep descent to the Colorado River, plunging 200 feet through Vishnu Schist along Devils Corkscrew, a dramatic series of switchbacks. The trail ends at the Bright Angel Suspension Bridge, which continues across the Colorado River to Bright Angel Campground and Phantom Ranch.

TRAILHEAD   The Bright Angel Trail starts next to Kolb's Studio, just west of the Bright Angel Lodge.

TRAIL INFO

RATING: Strenuous

HIKING TIME: 2–3 Days

DISTANCE: 15.6 miles, round-trip

ELEVATION CHANGE: 4,285 ft.

BRIGHT ANGEL TRAIL

Phantom Ranch

Bright Angel Campground

River Trail

Plateau Point

Tonto Trail

Devils Corkscrew

Indian Garden Campground

Maricopa Point

10

Yavapai Point

3

3 Mile Resthouse

1.5 Mile Resthouse

Bright Angel Lodge

6

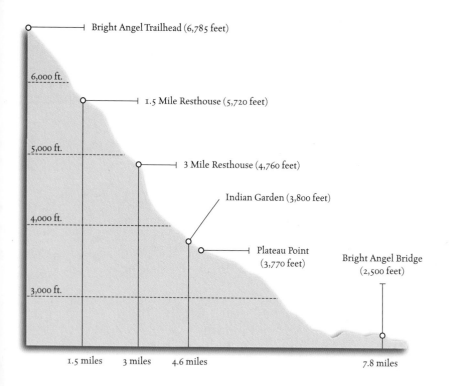

Bright Angel Trailhead (6,785 feet)

6,000 ft.

1.5 Mile Resthouse (5,720 feet)

5,000 ft.

3 Mile Resthouse (4,760 feet)

Indian Garden (3,800 feet)

4,000 ft.

Plateau Point
(3,770 feet)

Bright Angel Bridge
(2,500 feet)

3,000 ft.

1.5 miles   3 miles   4.6 miles   7.8 miles

BRIGHT ANGEL TRAIL

Devils Corkscrew, Bright Angel Trail

Plateau Point is one of the Inner Canyon's most stunning destinations. Perched 1,300 feet above the Colorado River, it treats hikers and mule riders to sweeping 360-degree views of some of the Canyon's most famous landmarks. If you're spending the night in Indian Garden Campground on the Bright Angel Trail, Plateau Point makes a fantastic sunrise or sunset destination. The 1.5-mile trail to Plateau Point is reached via the Tonto Trail near Indian Garden Campground. After crossing Garden Creek just below Indian Garden, follow the Tonto Trail west for roughly three quarters of a mile until reaching a fork: turn right and walk across the broad, flat platform to Plateau Point.

❧ SOUTH KAIBAB TRAIL ❧

SUMMARY   Steep and strenuous, the South Kaibab Trail is the South Rim's most direct route to the bottom of the Canyon. While most Inner Canyon trails follow side canyons, the South Kaibab Trail follows open ridgelines, providing spectacular views in all directions—great for day hikers. If you're day hiking, consider the popular 1.5-mile hike to Ooh-Aah Point (2–4 hours, round trip). The South Kaibab Trail ends at the Kaibab Suspension Bridge, which heads to Bright Angel Campground and Phantom Ranch. (If you're planning an overnight backpack to Bright Angel Campground or Phantom Ranch, consider hiking down the South Kaibab Trail and returning via the Bright Angel Trail, which is longer but slightly more gradual.) Note: there's no water on the South Kaibab Trail.

TRAILHEAD   The trail starts near Yaki Point (p.158), but private vehicles are not allowed at the trailhead. Free shuttles head to the South Kaibab Trailhead throughout the day from Canyon View Information Plaza. In the early morning, another shuttle departs from Bright Angel Lodge and the Backcountry Information Center. Check *The Guide* for seasonal schedules.

◆ TRAIL INFO ◆

RATING: Strenuous   **HIKING TIME:** 2 Days

DISTANCE: 14.6 miles, round-trip   **ELEVATION CHANGE:** 4,700 ft.

SOUTH KAIBAB TRAIL

Phantom
Ranch

Bright Angel
Campground

Plateau
Point

Bright Angel Trail

*The
Tipoff*

Tonto Trail

Skeleton
Point

O'Neil
Butte

Yavapai
Point

3

Cedar Ridge

Ooh Aah Point

16
Yaki Point

Rim Trail

Desert View Drive

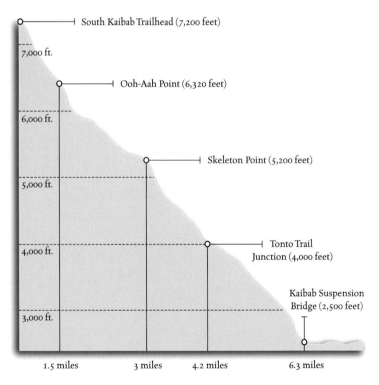

South Kaibab Trailhead (7,200 feet)

7,000 ft.

Ooh-Aah Point (6,320 feet)

6,000 ft.

Skeleton Point (5,200 feet)

5,000 ft.

Tonto Trail
Junction (4,000 feet)

4,000 ft.

Kaibab Suspension
Bridge (2,500 feet)

3,000 ft.

1.5 miles   3 miles   4.2 miles   6.3 miles

SOUTH KAIBAB TRAIL

South Kaibab Trail

⊰ HERMIT TRAIL ⊱

SUMMARY Although less famous than the popular Bright Angel Trail, the Hermit trail is one of the South Rim's finest hikes. Departing from Hermits Rest, it treats hikers to spectacular western vistas as it descends to the Colorado River in two steep drops. Though unmaintained, the Hermit Trail is generally in good shape with a few tricky but manageable washouts. Day hikers can head 2.5 miles to Santa Maria Spring (5–8 hours, round trip). The Hermit Trail ends along the banks of the Colorado River next to Hermit Rapid—one of the most thrilling rapids in Grand Canyon. If you're lucky, you'll catch a glimpse of river runners hooting and hollering as they barrel through the waves. Backpackers must camp at designated campsites at either Hermit Creek Campsite (located just west of the Hermit Trail along the Tonto Trail) or at Hermit Rapid.

TRAILHEAD The Hermit Trail starts west of Hermits Rest at the end of Hermit Road. Overnight hikers can park at the trailhead (you'll be given a code to open the gate to Hermit Road); day hikers can ride the free shuttle to Hermits Rest.

TRAIL INFO

RATING: Strenuous **HIKING TIME:** 2–3 Days
DISTANCE: 18.6 miles, round-trip **ELEVATION CHANGE:** 4,240 ft.

HERMIT TRAIL

Whites Butte

Travertine Canyon

Hermit
Rapid

Tonto Trail

Cathedral
Stairs

Yuma
Point

Hermit
Creek
Campsite

Breezy
Point

Eremita Mesa

Hermit Gorge

Pima
Point

14

Boucher Trail

Hermit Road

Hermits
Rest

15

Santa
Maria
Spring

Dripping Springs Trail

Waldron Trail

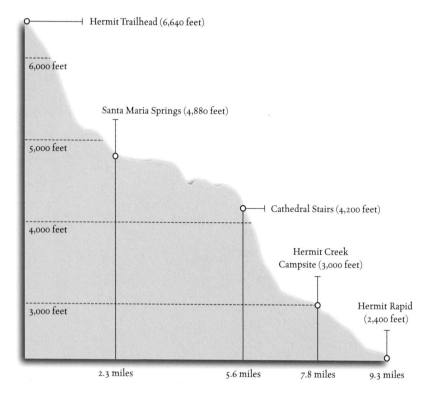

Hermit Trailhead (6,640 feet)

6,000 feet

Santa Maria Springs (4,880 feet)

5,000 feet

Cathedral Stairs (4,200 feet)

4,000 feet

Hermit Creek
Campsite (3,000 feet)

3,000 feet

Hermit Rapid
(2,400 feet)

2.3 miles   5.6 miles   7.8 miles   9.3 miles

HERMIT TRAIL

Hermit Trail

⊰ GRANDVIEW TRAIL ⊱

SUMMARY The Grandview Trail drops roughly 2,600 feet from Grandview Point to dramatic Grandview Mesa. It's one of the few Inner Canyon trails that doesn't descend all the way to the Colorado River. Although the entire Grandview Trail is much shorter than other South Rim Hikes, it's extremely steep. Energetic day hikers can head to the campground at Horseshoe Mesa (6–9 hours, round trip). Backpackers can camp on Horseshoe Mesa, but there are no water sources. All water must be hauled in. Several trails descend roughly 1,000 feet from Horseshoe Mesa to the Tonto Trail. If you're spending the night, a brief hike to the stunning overlook at the eastern tip of Horseshoe Mesa makes a great day trip. Note: There are many abandoned copper mines in the vicinity of Horseshoe Mesa. Do not enter abandoned mine shafts. They are extremely dangerous.

TRAILHEAD The Grandview Trail starts at Grandview Point, about 12 miles east of Grand Canyon Village on Desert View Drive. There is a parking area next to the trailhead.

TRAIL INFO

RATING: Strenuous **HIKING TIME:** 1–2 Days

DISTANCE: 6 miles, round-trip **ELEVATION CHANGE:** 2,500 ft.

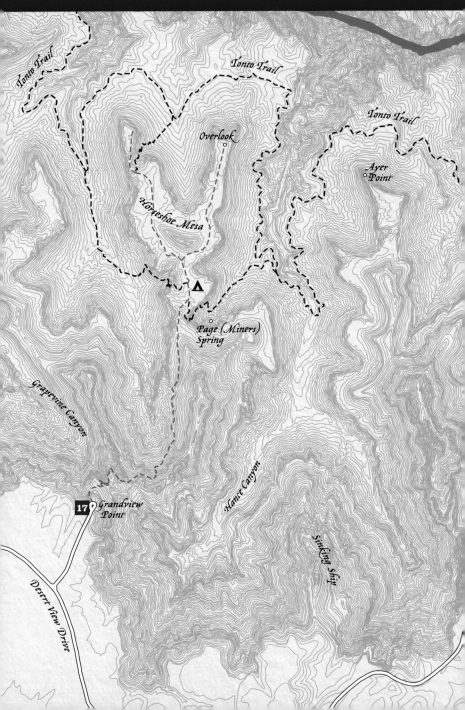

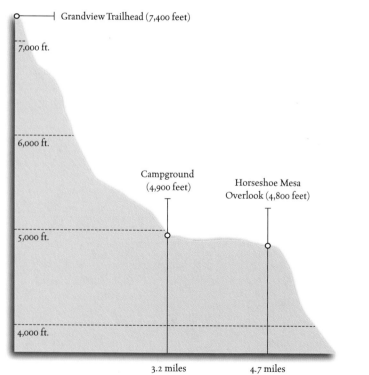

Grandview Trailhead (7,400 feet)

7,000 ft.

6,000 ft.

Campground
(4,900 feet)

Horseshoe Mesa
Overlook (4,800 feet)

5,000 ft.

4,000 ft.

3.2 miles

4.7 miles

GRANDVIEW TRAIL

THE COLORADO RIVER

⭑ ⭑ ⭑ ⭑ ⭑

Introduction 199
History 200
Sights. 214

COLORADO RIVER

THE COLORADO RIVER is the heart and soul of Grand Canyon. Without it, there would be no Grand Canyon, just another quiet stretch of land rolling through northern Arizona. Instead, the river has cut a mile into the surrounding landscape, exposed nearly two billion years worth of Earth's history, and flushed out over 1,000 cubic miles of eroded debris. The result is the single most impressive natural feature in North America.

As stunning as the view is from the rim, the view from the river is even more spectacular. Flowing downstream from Lees Ferry (just south of the Utah/Arizona border), the Colorado enters the most scenic stretch of whitewater in America. As the river cascades down a series of thrilling rapids, sheer cliffs rise up thousands of feet on either side. Twisting deep into the heart of the Canyon, the river exposes a dazzling natural world filled with towering rock formations, sandy beaches, dark caverns, and sparkling waterfalls. Side canyons spread out in all directions, channelling unlikely streams through the parched terrain. As the Colorado glides and swirls around sharp bends in the Canyon, cool shadows mingle with shimmering river light.

As the largest river in the Southwest, the Colorado is a river of liquid gold. Its water, delivered via massive aqueducts, allows millions of people to live in the desert and enables farmers to grow billions of dollars of food year-round. Although plugged by dams and reservoirs along much of its length, the Colorado flows free in Grand Canyon for 277 miles, providing river runners with some of the most spectacular river scenery in America.

Only 20,000 people—less than half of one percent of all park visitors—embark on a river trip through Grand Canyon each year. The number of river runners is limited by the park service to preserve the pristine wilderness at the bottom of the Canyon. Those lucky enough to witness Grand Canyon from the Colorado are filled with an overpowering sense of awe. Physically, the size of Canyon is humbling. Visually, it's one of the most dynamic places in the world, changing with the weather, the seasons, and the particular time of day. Even seasoned world travelers admit that a river trip through Grand Canyon is one of the most remarkable journeys on the planet.

NATURAL HISTORY

F ROM START TO finish, the Colorado River passes through some of the most beautiful and varied terrain in North America. Born in the deep gorges of the upper Rocky Mountains, it plunges head first down the pine-covered slopes to emerge in the desert Southwest. The river cuts through the wind-swept canyons of Utah, tears deep into the Grand Canyon, and then glides through the California desert. By the time it crosses the Mexican border to empty into the Gulf of California, the river has passed through seven western states and drained an area the size of Iraq.

The Colorado River is often referred to as the "Nile of America." At first glance, this comparison seems appropriate. Both rivers pass through vast desert regions and both sustain vast desert civilizations along the way. But despite these two basic similarities, the rivers share little else in common. In terms of size, the Colorado is a much smaller river, draining a quarter of the land that the Nile drains. In terms of length, the Colorado's 1,400 miles pales in comparison to the Nile's 4,000.

Even in America, the Colorado lacks many impressive statistics. It's not the longest river in America. Six other rivers are longer. Nor is it the biggest river in America. In terms of annual flow, the Colorado doesn't even rank in the top 25. But what the Colorado does have, and what makes it so remarkable, is the wildest and most terrifying elevation drop of any river in North America.

From its headwaters in the Rocky Mountains to the Gulf of California, the Colorado drops over 13,000 vertical feet. This steep drop, occurring over a rel-atively short distance, churns up a river that is fast and furious, dropping an aver-age of 7.7 feet per mile—25 times steeper than the mighty Mississippi. Because a river's erosive power increases exponentially with its speed, the Colorado would be a highly destructive river in any part of the world. But in the desert Southwest, a crumbling landscape filled with soft rocks and sparse vegetation, its erosive power is monumental.

As the Colorado enters the Southwest, it grinds away at the region's barren rocks, picking up tiny particles of sediment along the way. The more sediment the river picks up, the more abrasive it becomes. The more abrasive it becomes, the more sediment it picks up. This vicious cycle feeds on itself until the Colorado is, quite literally, a river of liquid sandpaper. Before massive dams plugged the Colorado, the river's sediment loads were phenomenal. Back then the Colorado carried an average of 235,000 tons of sediment through the Grand Canyon *each day*. "Too thick to drink, too thin to plow," was how one early explorer described it. The river's composition was often two parts sediment to one part water, and because the sediment had a high concentration of iron-oxide the virgin Colorado had a distinct reddish hue.

The virgin Colorado was also psychotically unpredictable. Early explorers often compared it to a bull. It was an "angry bull," a "blooded bull," and a "wild bull of destruction." The Colorado's flows in Grand Canyon varied anywhere between 3,000 and 200,000 cubic feet of water (90 to 6,000 tons) *per second*, sometimes within a matter of weeks. The largest flows occurred in the spring, when snowmelt from the Rocky Mountains set loose months of accumulated precipitation. In any given year, snowmelt accounts for over 70 percent of the river's flow.

The Colorado's spring floods were biblical in proportion. Roaring through the Southwest, they ripped out vegetation, eroded huge chunks of the riverbank, and tumbled 20-ton boulders like ice cubes. During these floods the river carried its heaviest sediment loads, devouring the landscape at an astonishing rate.

But by winter the Colorado would slow to a trickle and hover just above freezing—a stark contrast to summertime highs when the river often topped 80

SEDIMENT LOAD

The amount of sediment a river can carry increases to the sixth power of its speed. A river flowing at 2 mph will carry 64 times more sediment ($2^6=64$) than a river flowing at 1 mph ($1^6=1$). Likewise, a river flowing at 10 mph will carry 1 million times more sediment than a river flowing at 1 mph. During spring floods the virgin Colorado often flowed at speeds topping 40 mph, carrying up to 27 million tons of sediment through Grand Canyon *each day*. During these floods, Grand Canyon experienced its most intense erosion.

degrees. An entire ecosystem evolved to live in these harrowing conditions. The humpback chub, a fish found only in the Colorado, has a lifecycle timed to the river's wild temperature swings. It also has strong muscles and an uncanny sense of fluid dynamics to keep from washing away during spring floods. Plants were also influenced by the flooding; apache plume, mesquite, and catclaw acacia grew only above the flood zone.

As the Colorado travels to the sea, it passes through an amazing diversity of landscapes. In Grand Canyon alone, it encounters three of North America's four deserts. Vegetation typical of the Great Basin Desert, found in Nevada and western Utah, is visible from Lees Ferry to river mile 39. At river mile 39 the Colorado enters the northernmost outpost of the Sonoran Desert, covering much of Arizona, Southern California, and northern Mexico. At river mile 157 the Colorado enters the Mojave Desert, the smallest of the four deserts but home to such national treasures as Death Valley and Joshua Tree National Park.

The Colorado River in Grand Canyon is on average 300 feet wide and 25 feet deep. Within the Canyon the river is essentially a series of long pools interrupted by short, quick rapids. Although rapids only account for 10 percent of the Colorado's 277-mile length in Grand Canyon, they account for nearly half of its 2,000-foot elevation drop, and the velocity of water in rapids is up to 10 times greater than in the long pools in between. On most rivers, rapids form wherever the riverbed naturally drops. But in Grand Canyon rapids form next to side canyons where flash floods have dumped debris into the Colorado. The debris constricts the river, backs it up, and creates a steep drop-off—the rapid. Some of these rapids, which can drop up to 30 feet in a matter of seconds, are considered among the most thrilling whitewater on the planet.

CERTAIN DEATH

IN 1849 an Indian who spoke no English attempted to describe the Colorado River to would-be river runner William Manly. Using a stick to draw in the sand, he mapped the upper Colorado passing through mountains, valleys, and canyons. He then piled up stones to represent the deepest canyon of all. According to Manly, the Indian, "stood with one foot on each side of his river and put his hands on the stones and then raised them as high as he could, making a continued e-e-e-e-e as long as his breath would last, pointed to the canoe and made signs with his hands how it would roll and pitch in the rapids and finally capsize and throw us all out. He then made signs of death to show us that it was a fatal place. I understood perfectly from this that below the valley where we now were was a terrible {canyon}, much higher than any we had passed, and the rapids were not navigable with safety."

THE NEW COLORADO

ODAY, GRAND CANYON is an oasis of uninterrupted whitewater on a river plugged with dams. Below Grand Canyon, Hoover Dam holds back Lake Mead, the largest man-made lake in the Western Hemisphere. Above Grand Canyon, Glen Canyon Dam holds back Lake Powell, the second largest man-made lake in the Western Hemisphere. Almost all of the water that enters Grand Canyon now passes through the turbines at Glen Canyon Dam, a fact that has significantly altered the downstream ecology.

Since the floodgates at Glen Canyon Dam closed in 1963, the Colorado River in Grand Canyon has undergone a dramatic transformation. Its flow, temperature, and sediment load—the defining characteristics of the river—have all changed. Other than the path it follows, the new Colorado bears almost no resemblance to the pre-dam river.

Historically, the amount of water flowing through Grand Canyon was determined by the amount of precipitation that fell on the Colorado River Basin. Today, the amount of water flowing through Grand Canyon is determined by the engineers at Glen Canyon Dam. Maximum flows are capped at less than 10 percent of what they once were, and the massive spring floods that created much of Grand Canyon have been eliminated. This lack of flooding has created several problems. Most notably, much of the debris washed into the river through side canyons now lies dormant on the bottom of the river. Before the dam, spring floods cleared out the debris and washed it downstream.

Glen Canyon Dam smoothed out the river's seasonal flows, but daily flows became wildly erratic. The amount of water released from the dam is based on the region's fluctuating power demand, and during peak hours in the afternoon dam operators can charge twice as much for electricity as they can at night. When Glen Canyon Dam first opened, daily flows fluctuated anywhere between 3,000 and 31,500 cubic feet per second. Downstream, the river rose and fell like a toilet tank. Daily tides often topped 13 feet and beaches along the banks of the river eroded at an unnaturally high rate. In 1992 the Grand Canyon Protection Act was passed, requiring dam operators to smooth out releases to reduce beach erosion.

Glen Canyon Dam has also affected the Colorado's sediment load. Ninety percent of the sediment that used to enter Grand Canyon is now trapped behind Glen Canyon Dam, and each year Lake Powell fills up with more and more sediment—a problem that future generations will have to contend with. In the meantime, water drawn from Lake Powell enters Grand Canyon almost completely silt free.

DISAPPEARING BEACHES

BEFORE GLEN CANYON Dam was constructed in 1963, the banks of the Colorado in Grand Canyon were lined with hundreds of sandy beaches. Replenished each spring by the virgin Colorado's annual floods, the beaches provided valuable habitat for native species and were used as campsites by early river runners. But following the construction of Glen Canyon Dam, the river's sediment load in Grand Canyon was reduced by 80 percent, and the beaches started to erode. Adding to the problem were the dam's erratic releases, which were timed to coincide with daily fluctuations in power demand. The releases created huge tides that stripped additional sand from the beaches and flushed it out of Grand Canyon.

In 1992 President George Bush signed the Grand Canyon Protection Act, which ordered Glen Canyon Dam to operate in a way that protected and enhanced Grand Canyon National Park, including smoothing out daily releases. Maximum flows were capped at 26,000 cubic feet per second (cfs), and daily fluctuations were limited to 8,000 cfs.

Scientists were convinced that smoothed out flows would significantly reduce Grand Canyon beach erosion. But to their dismay, beach erosion contin-

streams—enough, theoretically, to replenish the beaches—was languishing at the bottom of the river. What Grand Canyon needed, the scientists concluded, was an old-fashioned flood to stir up the sediment and redeposit it on the riverbank.

In March 1996 Secretary of the Interior Bruce Babbitt turned the wheel at Glen Canyon Dam to release a controlled flood of 45,000 cfs. The flood churned up the river and created more than 50 new beaches. Within a year, however, many of those beaches had disappeared. The flood, it turned out, didn't so much create new beaches as wash existing beaches further downstream. Some scientists blamed the failure on the timing of the flood. Most tributary streams deposit new sediment into Grand Canyon during the rainy summer season. But the flood was conducted in the spring when much of the new sediment had already been washed out of the Canyon. In 2004 a second controlled flood was released in November, when the river contained significantly more sediment. The long-term effects of this flood are still being monitored, but initial results appear to be disappointing.

In the end, the controlled floods stirred up as much controversy as they did sediment. And as the Southwest continues to grow, each drop of water in Lake Powell becomes more valuable than ever. Many oppose sacrificing this water to test unproven theories, but something needs to be done before Grand Canyon's beaches disappear for good.

The water released by Glen Canyon Dam is drawn from the chilly depths of Lake Powell, entering Grand Canyon at a constant 45 degrees. Not surprisingly, this frigid water has significantly altered the Colorado's ecosystem. For millions of years fish native to the Colorado had their life cycles timed to the river's wild temperatures swings. They could survive in the cold winter water, but needed warm summer water to spawn. Now that the warm water has disappeared, Grand Canyon's native fish have been forced to spawn in a handful of smaller tributaries.

As spawning grounds have disappeared, so have the fish. Of the Canyon's eight native fish, five are now extinct. Among those lost is the impressive six-foot Colorado squawfish. The humpback chub, one of the few species that remains, has been pushed to the brink of extinction. Scientists estimate that there are fewer than 2,000 humpback chub left. Adding to the problem are non-native sport fish that have been introduced to the river. New arrivals such as trout, catfish, and carp thrive in the chilly water and compete with native fish for resources.

Although the new Colorado has wrecked havoc with native fish populations, it has allowed other life forms to thrive. The cool, clear, sediment-free water allows sunlight to penetrate its depths, fostering the growth of algae. The abundance of algae has formed the foundation of a healthy food chain and turned the river a gorgeous shade of green.

Even the riverbank has undergone a major ecological change. For millions of years the annual spring floods scoured the sides of the river. Now that flooding has been eliminated, a dense thicket of plants has taken up residence in the previous flood zone. This explosion of plants has led to a dramatic increase in animal habitat and biodiversity.

Glen Canyon Dam completely changed the downstream ecology of the Colorado River. Although many conservationists would like to see the dam destroyed and the Colorado returned to its natural state, Glen Canyon Dam is unlikely to be decommissioned anytime soon. It provides valuable water and electricity to a desert region starved for both. And although the river's ecology has been shaken up, there have been many tangible improvements. The new river supports more plants and animals than the old one did, and its regulated flow allows hundreds of river trips to safely navigate Grand Canyon each year

HUMAN HISTORY

ALTHOUGH THE COLORADO River is often hard to see from the rim of Grand Canyon, the Canyon itself is clearly visible from space. Equally impressive is the view from space at night when the desert is filled with dense clusters of light—the booming cities of the Southwest. Over the past few decades, millions of people have flocked to cities like Phoenix, Tucson and Las Vegas, eager to leave cold winters elsewhere behind. This phenomenal migration, continuing today, would have been impossible without water from the Colorado River. In a land of little rain, the Colorado is a river of liquid gold that has allowed the Southwest to flourish.

Today, billions of dollars of agriculture, billions of dollars of industry, and millions of daily lives revolve around the Colorado River. Never before in history have so many people and such an enormous economy become so dependent on a single source of water. It is, without question, the most important natural resource in the West. But it is a limited resource, and huge demands have been placed on it. Today its flow is so regulated and its water so overused that not a single drop reaches the sea. And as the Southwest continues to grow, so do demands on the river. As a result, the Colorado has become one of the most argued over, litigated, politicized, and controversial rivers in the world.

The first attempt to tap the Colorado was a disaster. In the late 1800s a developer named Charles Rockwood realized that, given a steady source of water, the California desert could be turned into an agricultural paradise. If the Colorado River could be tapped and controlled, farmers could grow crops an amazing 12 months of the year.

In 1901 a diversion channel was cut into the Colorado. Overnight, California's previously bone-dry Imperial Valley became one of the most productive agricultural regions on the planet. But because the Colorado ran thick with sediment, the diversion channel soon silted up and the Colorado jumped its banks, tearing off in a totally new direction. Instead of draining into the Gulf of California, the Colorado flowed into the middle of Southern California. For the next three years the river dumped its entire flow into the desert lowland area known as the Salton Sink. By the time engineers were able to redirect the river, an inland sea roughly one-third the size of Rhode Island had formed. The Salton Sea is still there today.

The Colorado was a force to be reckoned with, but there was too much money at stake to give up trying to tame it. The arid West was on the verge of a massive expansion, and savvy politicians realized that its future was linked directly to water in the Colorado River. In the end, there was only one solution: build a massive dam that could regulate the Colorado, hold back its floods, and store them in a reservoir for later use.

In 1933 construction began on Hoover Dam. It was the biggest dam the world had ever seen. It tamed the Colorado, generated an enormous amount of electricity, and allowed the desert to bloom. Hoover Dam was such a resounding success that the government agency responsible for its creation, the Bureau of Reclamation, soon became the golden child of American politics. Using the momentum generated by Hoover Dam, the Bureau set off on a wild tear of dam building that lasted for the next 30 years.

The construction of so many expensive dams created huge economic windfalls in the states where they were built. Across the country dam building was a politically charged process, but on the Colorado River the issue was even more complex. In 1922 a document called the Colorado River Compact had been drafted to allocate water from the Colorado River to the seven Colorado River Basin states. The Compact divided the region into an Upper Basin and a Lower Basin, each receiving 7.5 million acre feet of water per year. It was up to the states to figure out how to divvy up the water after that.

Not surprisingly, the Compact set off vicious inter-state water wars. Water was essential to each state's growth, and there simply wasn't enough to go around. The only way for a state to secure long-term water rights was to put that water to use before another state did. The result was the hasty construction of massive multi-billion dollar irrigation projects that, in reality, made little practical sense. In a few short decades, 19 dams had been built on the Colorado and its tributaries and the river had been sucked dry.

Despite these problems, the Bureau of Reclamation continued to push for new dams. In 1963 Glen Canyon Dam was constructed to the furor of conservationists. When two more dams were proposed within Grand Canyon, the conservationists went wild. Led by David Brower of the Sierra Club, they used congressional hearings, letter writing campaigns, and modern media savvy to defeat the dams (p.98).

The Bureau's defeat in Grand Canyon signaled a dramatic shift in popular opinion. Throughout much of the 20th century, dams had been viewed as glorious symbols of progress. But as the environmental movement took hold, many people viewed dams as hulking symbols of man's interference with nature. Before long, the era of massive dam building was brought to a halt.

The media blitz that defeated the dams also focused a tremendous amount of attention on the Colorado River in Grand Canyon. Soon, many ordinary people wanted to see it for themselves. Prior to 1950, fewer than 100 people had paddled through Grand Canyon. By 1970, roughly 15,000 people were making the trip each year. To reduce crowding, the park service began limiting the number of river runners allowed in Grand Canyon. Today roughly 20,000 people run the Colorado through Grand Canyon each year. And while the river as a whole is submerged in controversy, the uninterrupted stretch of whitewater in Grand Canyon remains one of the most rugged and beautiful places in the world.

THE COLORADO RIVER COMPACT

IN 1922 DELEGATES from seven western states gathered outside Santa Fe, New Mexico, to allocate water from the Colorado River. Their negotiations resulted in the Colorado River Compact. At the time, it was hailed as a "Constitution for the West." In reality, it was one of the most poorly conceived documents in the history of American politics.

The Compact "solved" the issue of water ownership by splitting the Colorado Basin into two: an Upper Basin (Utah, Wyoming, Colorado, New Mexico) and a Lower Basin (California, Arizona, Nevada). Of the estimated 17 million acre feet of water flowing through the Colorado each year, each basin would receive 7.5 million acre feet. The Compact left it up to the states to decide how the water would be divided after that. Not surprisingly, the Compact touched off vicious inter-state water wars. Tensions flared and relationships were bruised, but the worst was yet to come.

In 1953 the government admitted that there was a fatal flaw in the Colorado River Compact. The Compact had overestimated the river's annual flow by roughly 3 million acre feet. States that had fought tooth and nail over every last drop of the Colorado River were now faced with the gut wrenching fact that their figures were all wrong. The water rights wars were thrown into turmoil. They remain in turmoil to this day.

THE COLORADO RIVER
in
GRAND CANYON

Vermillion Cliffs

Kanab Plateau

Lava Falls

HIDDEN PASSAGE

Grand Wash Cliffs

Shivwits Plateau

8

7

6

National
Canyon

Hava
India
Reser

Whitmore
Wash

Havasu Canyon

Hualapai
Indian
Reservation

Diamond Creek

Marble Canyon

Lake Powell

Paria River

1 Glen Canyon Dam

2 Lees Ferry

Shinumo Creek

3

North Canyon

Marble Canyon

Navajo Indian Reservation

Kanab Canyon

Redwall Cavern

Trinity Canyon

Saddle Canyon

4

Blacktail Canyon

Phantom Ranch

Bright Angel Point

Nankoweap

Grand Canyon Village

Desert View

Little Colorado River

Coconino Plateau

Elves Chasm

Carbon Canyon

San Francisco Peaks

1 Glen Canyon Dam

This massive dam, located 15 river miles north of Grand Canyon, holds back Lake Powell—the largest man-made reservoir in the western hemisphere, capable of holding over eight *trillion* gallons of water. Glen Canyon Dam is 710 feet tall, 300 feet thick at the base, and contains over 4.9 million cubic yards of cement. It took seven years to build and cost $272 million in 1963 dollars. If the dam's eight generators operated at full capacity, the dam could release 15 million gallons of water a minute and generate roughly 1.3 million kilowatts of electricity.

Since Glen Canyon Dam went into operation in 1963, it has completely changed the characteristics of the Colorado River in Grand Canyon. Water released from Glen Canyon Dam is drawn from the chilly depths of Lake Powell, and it enters Grand Canyon at a constant 45°F. Before the dam, river temperatures often topped 80°F in the summer. The new, frigid water has radically altered the downstream ecology, and the filtering effect of Glen Canyon Dam has created a river that, unlike the pre-dam Colorado, is remarkably clear and silt-free.

Many conservationists loathe Glen Canyon Dam. In addition to the ecological changes it has wrought, the dam flooded Glen Canyon—by many accounts one of the most beautiful places in the Southwest. Supporters of the dam claim that Lake Powell is equally beautiful. Furthermore, many previously inaccessible reaches of Glen Canyon can now be reached by motorboat. But most importantly, Glen Canyon Dam supplies water and power to an arid region starved for both.

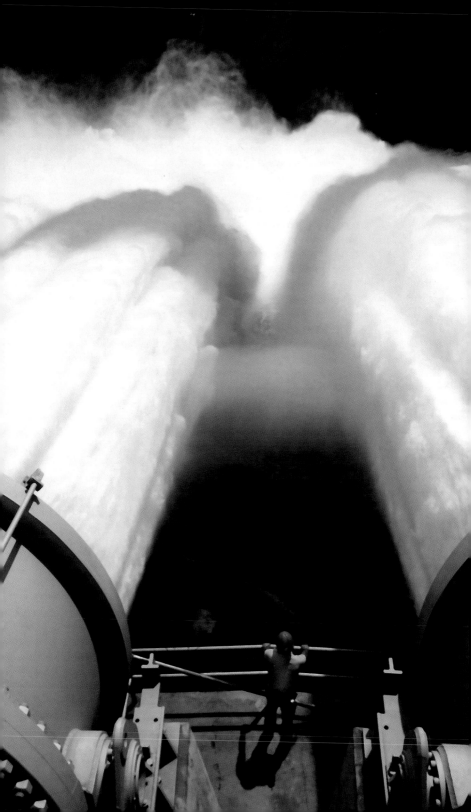

2 Lees Ferry (river mile 0)

Lees Ferry is the official launching point for every Grand Canyon river trip. It's the first spot on the Colorado River north of Grand Canyon accessible by road. (The next spot on the Colorado accessible by road is Diamond Creek, 225 miles downstream.) Lees Ferry is also the official boundary between the Upper and Lower Colorado River Basins, as set forth by the 1922 Colorado River Compact.

In 1776 Silvestre Vélez de Escalante, a Spanish missionary who became the first white person to set eyes on Lees Ferry, commented that, "It has an agreeably confused appearance." Despite being "agreeably confused," the gently sloping shores made it the only viable river crossing for hundreds of miles. For years Lees Ferry was known as Paria Crossing, named after the Paria River that empties into the Colorado a short distance downstream. Then, in 1872, a Mormon named John D. Lee established a permanent ferry service here. A few years earlier, Lee had participated in the Mountain Meadows Massacre, in which a group of Mormons slaughtered a wagon train of 120 pioneers on their way to California. In 1870 Lee was excommunicated from the Mormon Church. With the law at his back, Lee fled to Grand Canyon. But just two years after establishing Lees Ferry, he was captured and brought to trial. In 1877 Lee was executed by firing squad at Mountain Meadows. The ferry service continued to operate until 1928, when a ferry carrying a Model T capsized and killed all three people aboard. The following year Navajo Bridge was constructed a few miles downstream.

3 Marble Canyon (river miles 0–61)

Marble Canyon gives river runners their first taste of the power and beauty of Grand Canyon. Its steep, narrow walls offer dramatic scenery broken up by dozens of exciting rapids. Ironically, there's no marble in Marble Canyon. The name was given by John Wesley Powell (p.85), who thought the sedimentary rocks—polished smooth by muddy river water—resembled marble.

In the 1960s the U.S. Bureau of Reclamation wanted to build a dam at river mile 39. Had the dam been built, the upper reaches of Marble Canyon would have been flooded, but public pressure ultimately defeated the Bureau's plan.

WE HAVE CUT through the sandstones and limestones met in the upper part of the canyon, and through one great bed of marble a thousand feet in thickness. In this, great numbers of caves are hollowed out, and carvings are seen which suggest architectural forms, though on a scale so grand that architectural terms belittle them. As this great bed forms a distinctive feature of the canyon, we call it Marble Canyon.

— John Wesley Powell

"The water sweeps rapidly in this elbow of river, and has cut its way under the rock, excavating a vast half-circular chamber, which, if utilized for a theater, would give seating to 50,000 people. Objection might be raised against it, however, for at high water the floor is covered with a raging flood."

—John Wesley Powell

Redwall Cavern

Carbon Canyon

Saddle Canyon

4 Nankoweap (river mile 53)

Nankoweap is considered by many to be Marble Canyon's most beautiful stretch. In addition to spectacular scenery, this graceful bend in the river offers famous archaeological sites, pristine camping, and spectacular hiking nearby.

The origin of the name Nankoweap is a bit of a mystery. Some scholars believe the word is derived from a Paiute phrase meaning "Place Where Two Tribes Fought." Others believe the phrase means "Place That Echoes." What *is* known is that Nankoweap was home to an Ancestral Puebloan settlement hundreds of years ago. These ancient people, predecessors of the modern Hopi and Navajo tribes, farmed the fertile delta at Nankoweap and built granaries (stone storage compartments) in the cliffs above.

AND WHAT A world of grandeur is spread before us! Below is the canyon through which the Colorado runs . . . Away to the west are lines of cliffs and ledges of rock—not such ledges as the reader may have seen where they quarryman splits his blocks, but ledges from which the gods might quarry mountains . . .

—John Wesley Powell

Nankoweap

Trinity Canyon

Shinumo Creek

Elves Chasm

Blacktail Canyon

Deer Creek Falls

"The clouds are children of the heavens, and when they play among the rocks they lift them to the region above."

—John Wesley Powell

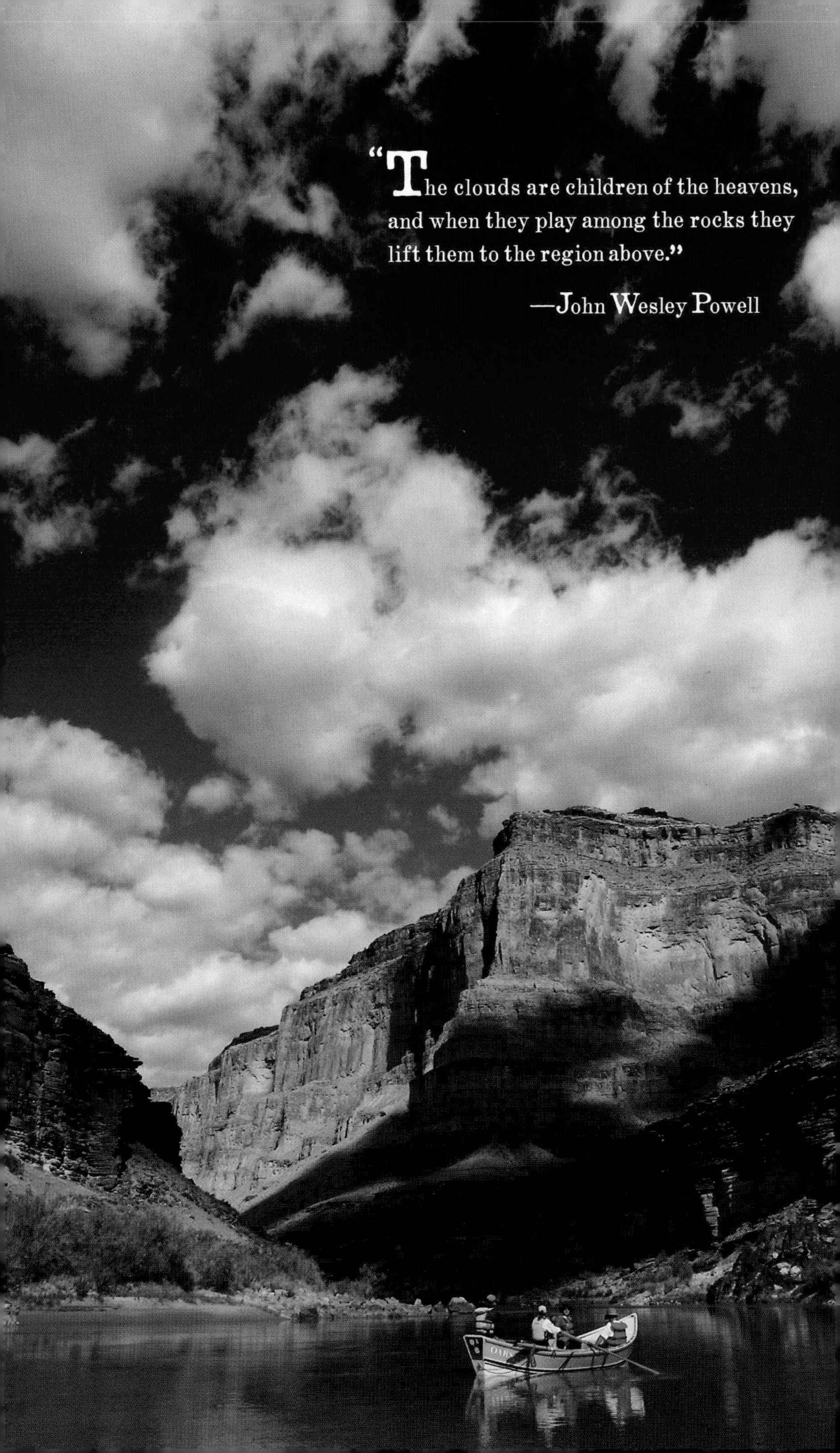

5 Kanab Canyon (river mile 143)

Kanab Canyon is one of Grand Canyon's largest and most beautiful side canyons. It was named by John Wesley Powell after the Paiute word for "willow." In 1872 Powell and his men ended their second Colorado River expedition here, hiking out of the Canyon to the North Rim. One year earlier, two prospectors had discovered trace amounts of gold in Kanab Canyon, setting off a minor gold rush that brought hundreds of fortune seekers here. The gold rush—which lasted all of four months—ended when the eager prospectors finally accepted the fact that there were no rich strikes in Kanab Canyon.

THE CREVICES ARE usually narrow above and, by erosion of the streams, wider below, forming a network of caves, each cave having a narrow, winding skylight up through the rocks. Wherever we look there is but a wilderness of rocks—deep gorges where the rivers are lost below cliffs and towers and pinnacles, and ten thousand strangely carved forms in every direction...

—John Wesley Powell

6 Havasu Canyon (river mile 157)

The beauty of Grand Canyon is stunning, but the beauty of Havasu Canyon seems almost hallucinatory. This secluded oasis—the most abundant side stream in Grand Canyon—is part tropical paradise, part Southwestern dreamscape. A well-worn path heads up Havasu Canyon from the river, revealing shockingly turquoise water tumbling over pink rocks in a series of tranquil pools, each one more beautiful than the last. No matter how far up the path you go, you'll be greeted with some of the most incredible scenery in the Southwest.

Havasu Canyon is located on the Havasupai Indian Reservation. Follow the path up Havasu Canyon 10 miles and you'll reach the village of Supai, home to about 400 Havasupai Indians. *Havasupai*, loosely translated, means "People of the Blue Green Water." Supai's world famous waterfalls draw several thousand visitors a year, but the village, located 2,000 feet below the rim, is only accessible by foot, mule, or helicopter (p.286). It's unrealistic to hike from the river to Supai and back in a single day, but Beaver Falls (located about four miles up the trail) is a beautiful waterfall that makes a good destination for strong day hikers.

Although Havasu Canyon only receives nine inches of rain a year, it drains a 3,000 square-mile basin. That drainage, combined with many springs, provides Havasu Creek with an average of 38 million gallons of water a day. The lurid blue water is due to a light coating of travertine—calcium carbonate leached from nearby rocks—on the riverbed, which gives the water its otherworldly hue.

Beaver Falls, Havasu Canyon

7 National Canyon (river mile 166)

National Canyon is one of many exquisite side canyons branching off from the Colorado River. These canyons, carved out over millions of years by flash floods roaring down from the rim, offer some of the most amazing scenery in Grand Canyon. Their walls have been sculpted and polished in an endless variety of patterns, alternately catching and concealing the sunlight throughout the day. Many of these side canyons are accessible only from the river, making them the exclusive domain of river runners. Some go on for miles, offering incredible hiking that many river runners consider to be the best part of their trip.

THE GORGE IS black and narrow below, red and gray and flaring above, with crags and angular projections on the walls, which, cut in many places by side canyons, seem to be a vast wilderness of rocks ... and ever as we go there is some new pinnacle or tower, some crag or peak, some distant view of the upper plateau, some strangely shaped rock, or some deep, narrow side canyon.

—John Wesley Powell

Matkatamiba Canyon

Matkatamiba Canyon

"What a conflict of water and fire there must have been here! Just imagine a river of molten rock running down into a river of melted snow. What a seething and boiling of the waters; what clouds of steam rolled into the heavens."

—John Wesley Powell

8 Lava Falls (river mile 179)

Lava Falls is one of the most challenging, terrifying, and thrilling rapids in Grand Canyon. It drops 13 feet in a matter of seconds, providing river runners with a rip-roaring ride—regardless of whether or not you stay inside your boat. Lava Falls is also the last major rapid conquered on most river trips. It's the grand finale after a symphony of singular sights.

Lava Falls is named for the nearby lava flows that have tumbled over the rim several times over the past 2 million years, accounting for the dark-colored basalt on the north side of the river. Roughly 1.6 million years ago, a nearby volcanic eruption sent four cubic miles of lava tumbling down to the Colorado River. When the lava cooled, it plugged the Canyon and formed a dam at least 2,300 feet high, creating a reservoir that took 22 years to fill and stretched all the way back to Moab, Utah.

Lava Falls shows mercy to no man, as demonstrated in 1989 when the rapids flipped a boat carrying Hollywood heavyweights Tom Cruise, Jeffrey Katzenberg, and Don Simpson. In the late 1980s, private Grand Canyon "power trips" became popular among Tinseltown titans and movie execs. The luxury on these trips was so extravagant, so over the top, so beyond *anything* the Canyon had ever seen that they are still talked about to this day. As the moguls conquered the rapids, extra supply rafts tagged along carrying gourmet food, wine, white linens, fine china, assistants, and private chefs. At night, candlelight dinners were served on the banks of the Colorado, featuring delicacies such as caviar and live lobster.

Lava Falls

THE NORTH RIM

⭐ ⭐ ⭐ ⭐ ⭐

Introduction 253
Basics 254
Map 258
Sights 259
Hiking 264

North Rim

ALTHOUGH THE NORTH RIM only lies 10 miles north of the South Rim as the crow flies, those of us confined to the ground have to drive 200 miles *around* Grand Canyon to get there. Make no mistake, the North Rim is remote. The closest major airport, Las Vegas' McCarran, is 280 miles to the southwest, and traveling to the North Rim means driving through one of the least densely populated places in the continental United States. As a result, fewer than one in ten Grand Canyon visitors ever makes it to the North Rim. But those who do are rewarded with some of Grand Canyon's most spectacular views—with one-tenth the crowds.

The North Rim is 1,000 feet higher than the South Rim, resulting in cooler temperatures and 60 percent more precipitation. Because of the cool and wet climate, the North Rim is covered in alpine forests of spruce, fir, and aspen, giving it a feel more like the Rockies than the desert Southwest. During summer heat spells when the South Rim is sweltering, the North Rim enjoys balmy afternoons and mild summer nights. Winters, on the other hand, bring so much snow that AZ-67—the only road to the North Rim—is forced to shut down. Only cross country skiers and snowshoers are allowed in the park during this time.

The hub of all activity on the North Rim is Grand Canyon Lodge (p.260), located at the southern terminus of AZ-67. The lodge offers overnight accommodations on the rim, but even if you're not a guest you can relax on the open-air back porch or dine in the upscale restaurant, both of which offer spectacular Canyon views. A short distance away is the pristine North Rim Campground, which fills up fast in the summer. Both the lodge and the campground are located within walking distance of Bright Angel Point (p.259), the North Rim's most popular overlook. A lazy drive along Cape Royal Road, meanwhile, brings you to even more spectacular views at Cape Royal and Point Imperial along the Walhalla Plateau (p.262).

The North Rim doesn't have much in the way of restaurants or gift shops, but that's all part of its charm. Visitors here are more interested in the rugged scenery and plentiful day hikes along the rim. If you're looking for a challenging overnight hike, the North Kaibab Trail (p.272) descends 14 miles to Bright Angel Campground and Phantom Ranch. And if you're really looking to test your backpacking mettle, head 30 miles to the northwest to the exceptionally beautiful—and exceptionally challenging—Thunder River Trail (p.276), one of the best hikes in Grand Canyon.

North Rim
BASICS

GETTING TO THE NORTH RIM

There's only one road to the North Rim: AZ-67, which heads south from the small town of Jacob Lake on I-89A. From Jacob Lake follow AZ-67 south 44 miles to Grand Canyon Lodge. No buses or trains run to the North Rim, but there is a trans-Canyon shuttle (see below). The closest major airports are located in Las Vegas, Nevada (280 miles distant), and Salt Lake City, Utah (380 miles distant).

RIM TO RIM SHUTTLE

From mid-May through mid-October, the Trans Canyon Shuttle runs daily routes between the North Rim and the South Rim. The shuttle leaves the North Rim at 7 a.m. and arrives at the South Rim around noon. It then leaves the South Rim at 1:30 p.m. and arrives back at the North Rim around 6:30 p.m. Cost: $70 one-way, $130 round-trip. Reservations are necessary (928-638-2820).

INFORMATION

The best resource for North Rim information is the North Rim edition of the park's free newspaper, *The Guide*. Copies of *The Guide* are handed out at the park entrance station. Information is also available at the **North Rim Visitor Center**, located adjacent to Grand Canyon Lodge, which also features maps, brochures, exhibits, and a bookstore.

WHEN TO GO

Summer is the busiest time on the North Rim, but crowds rarely get excessive. Fall brings changing leaves and crisp temperatures, making it one of the best times to visit. North Rim facilities shut down in mid-October, but the park remains open until winter's first heavy snow shuts down AZ-67 (anytime from October–December). In the winter the North Rim is open only to adventurous snowshoers and cross country skiers. The park reopens in the spring when the snow melts, but temperatures on the North Rim can stay chilly through June.

FEES

The North Rim entrance fee (which also gives you access to the South Rim), is $25 per vehicle or $12 per pedestrian, motorcycle rider, or cyclist. Admission is good for seven days. Another option is the America The Beautiful Pass ($80), which gives you unlimited access to all U.S. national parks and federal recreation lands for one full year.

WEATHER

Due to its high elevation, the North Rim is about five to ten degrees cooler than the South Rim and receives significantly more precipitation. Afternoon showers are common during monsoon season (July, August, early September), and deep winter snows sometimes top 10 feet. Spring and fall can be dry and delightful, but the weather during these times is often unpredictable—be prepared for sudden changes. Nights often drop below freezing in the spring and fall.

WHAT TO BRING

Unlike the bustling South Rim, shopping at the North Rim is very limited. When planning a trip to the North Rim, make extra sure you've packed everything you need. Warm clothes and rain gear (both of which are essential at any time of the year on the North Rim) should be at the top your packing list.

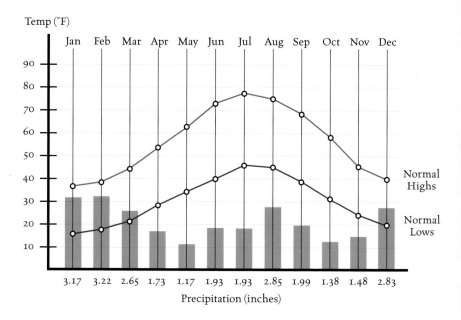

LODGING

GRAND CANYON LODGE

This rustic lodge, perched right on the rim of the Canyon, offers the only overnight accommodations on the North Rim. Rooms are often booked months in advance during the summer, but same-day reservations due to cancellations are sometimes available (888-297-2757, www.grandcanyonnorthrim.com). Four types of rooms are offered: **Frontier Cabins** ($100) offer one double bed, one twin bed, ¾ bath. **Pioneer Cabins** ($110) offer two bedrooms—one double bed, three twin beds—separated by ¾ bath. **Western Cabins** ($120) offer two queen beds, full bathroom, and a porch; four cabins offer rim views ($130), but they are booked as much as two years in advance. **Motel Room**s ($100) offer one queen bed and a full bath.

CAMPING

NORTH RIM CAMPGROUND

This pristine campground, located about a mile northwest of Grand Canyon Lodge, has about 90 sites, four with Canyon views. Rate: $15 ($20 for the four sites with Canyon views); backpackers and other visitors without cars only pay $4 per night. Reservations, which can be made up to six months in advance, are highly recommended (877-444-6777, www.recreation.gov).

DINING

GRAND CANYON LODGE DINING ROOM

Offers fine dining on the North Rim with tremendous views of the Canyon. Open breakfast, lunch, and dinner. Dinner reservations required (928-638-2612).

DELI IN THE PINES

This standard deli is located on the west side of Grand Canyon Lodge. Open breakfast, lunch, and dinner.

ROUGHRIDER SALOON

Gourmet coffee shop with pastries by day, well-stocked bar by night. Located on the east side of Grand Canyon Lodge.

**For additional lodging and camping options near
the North Rim, visit www.jameskaiser.com**

GETTING AROUND THE NORTH RIM

BY CAR
Having a car is essential if you plan to explore any part of the North Rim not within walking distance of Grand Canyon Lodge (Point Imperial Road, Cape Royal Road, etc.).

BY SHUTTLE
The early morning North Rim Hiker Shuttle runs between Grand Canyon Lodge and the North Kaibab Trailhead. Cost: $5 for the first person, $2 each additional person. Check *The Guide* for times. Tickets available at Grand Canyon Lodge.

ON FOOT
Bright Angel Point (p.259) and the Transept Trail (p.264) are both within walking distance of Grand Canyon Lodge.

BY BICYCLE
Bicycles are allowed on all paved and dirt roads on the North Rim (unless otherwise posted), but they are prohibited from all other park trails.

SERVICES

NORTH RIM GENERAL STORE
This small store, located near the entrance to the North Rim Campground, sells basic groceries and camping supplies. Generally open 8 a.m.–8 p.m.

GAS
There's a small gas station near the North Rim Campground off AZ-67.

LAUNDRY & SHOWERS
Coin-operated laundry and showers are located at the North Rim Campground.

ENTERTAINMENT

RANGER PROGRAMS
Free ranger programs are offered daily on topics including history, geology, wildlife and more. Check *The Guide* for exact times and locations.

MULE TRIPS
Day trips are offered along the rim and partway down the North Kaibab Trail. One-hour trips ($30), half-day trips ($65), and full-day trips ($125, including lunch) are offered. For more information visit the Grand Canyon Trail Rides desk at Grand Canyon Lodge (435-679-8665).

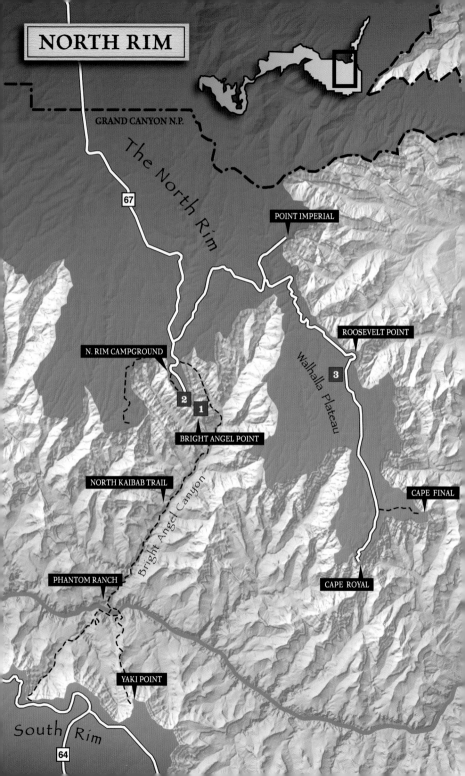

NORTH RIM

GRAND CANYON N.P.

The North Rim

67

POINT IMPERIAL

ROOSEVELT POINT

N. RIM CAMPGROUND

Walhalla Plateau

3

2 1

BRIGHT ANGEL POINT

NORTH KAIBAB TRAIL

Bright Angel Canyon

CAPE FINAL

PHANTOM RANCH

CAPE ROYAL

YAKI POINT

South Rim

64

1 Bright Angel Point

This popular viewpoint, located southeast of Grand Canyon Lodge, is accessible via a short paved path that begins to the left of the North Rim Visitor Center, just beyond the cabin area. After an initial drop at the start, the trail stays relatively flat with only a few mild ups and downs. Dramatic views of Roaring Springs Canyon unfold to your left, and towards the end of the trail you'll come to a small bridge that takes you to Bright Angel Point. The point itself is fenced in by a small metal railing. Interpretive signs point out famous Canyon landmarks visible from Bright Angel Point. The rocky outcrop directly behind the observation platform is a popular place to take in the view, but use caution if you climb onto the outcrop—there are many steep drop-offs.

Gazing across the Canyon from Bright Angel Point, the walls of the South Rim appear nearly vertical, while the walls of the North Rim gradually recede from the Colorado River. This is due to varying rates of erosion. Both the North Rim and the South Rim are tilted slightly to the south, so any precipitation that falls on the North Rim flows *into* the Canyon while precipitation that falls on the South Rim flows *away* from the Canyon. Because the walls of the North Rim receive so much more runoff, they have eroded horizontally up to 10 times faster than the walls of the South Rim.

Beyond the South Rim, punctuating the southeastern horizon, are the San Francisco Mountains. On clear days you can make out Humphrey's Peak, the highest point in Arizona at 12,643 feet.

2 Grand Canyon Lodge

Perched right on the rim, Grand Canyon Lodge offers tremendous views of the Canyon from its two open-air terraces. During the day, these terraces are a great place to relax and take in the views; at night a crackling fire is often built in the stone fireplace on the eastern terrace. Sandwiched between the terraces is the indoor Sun Room, where comfy leather chairs face giant picture windows that gaze out over the Canyon. Just up the steps from the Sun Room is the Grand Canyon Lodge Dining Room, an upscale restaurant that also features giant picture windows with spectacular views.

The original Grand Canyon Lodge, built in 1928, was the brainchild of Stephen Mather, the first director of the National Park Service. In the 1920s Mather championed the construction of grand lodges in then-remote western parks to help lure visitors. Designed by Gilbert Stanley Underwood, the architect behind Yosemite's famous Ahwahnee Hotel, the original Grand Canyon Lodge was built out of native ponderosa pines and Kaibab limestone. But just four years after it opened, a fire burned down the original structure. Only the small buildings on either side of the structure were spared, and they are still in use today. The current lodge was built in 1936. When completed it boasted improvements such as steel beams (as opposed to flammable pine beams) and sloped roofs to deflect the North Rim's heavy snows. Today Grand Canyon Lodge is a Registered National Historic Landmark.

3 Walhalla Plateau

This dramatic peninsula of land, jutting out 15 miles into the Canyon just east of Bright Angel Point, contains some of the North Rim's finest and most accessible viewpoints. To get there by car from Grand Canyon Lodge, drive north three miles on AZ-67 and turn right onto Fuller Canyon Road. Soon the road forks—head left to go to Point Imperial, head right to go to Cape Royal.

At 8,803 feet, Point Imperial is the highest vantage point in Grand Canyon. The dramatic spire to the east marks the top of Mount Hayden (8,372 feet).

Sixteen-mile Cape Royal Road heads to the southern tip of Walhalla Plateau. Along the way you'll pass a number of fine viewpoints including Vista Encantada, which has picnic tables, and Roosevelt Point, which provides a rare glimpse of the confluence of the Colorado and Little Colorado Rivers. Cape Final (p.266) is a short, highly recommended day hike that starts six miles past Roosevelt Point. Continuing on, the road passes Walhalla Overlook. Across the road from the overlook are the remains of a six-room Ancestral Puebloan pueblo, thought to have been inhabited sometime around A.D. 1050. A large parking area marks the end of Cape Royal Road. From the parking area a short paved trail passes by Angel's Arch—a natural arch that frames a view of the Colorado River—en route to Cape Royal, the southernmost viewpoint on the North Rim, which provides sweeping views of the Canyon.

⊷ TRANSEPT TRAIL ⊶

SUMMARY   The Transept Trail is an easy, charming stroll along the dramatic edge of Transept Canyon. Connecting Grand Canyon Lodge with the North Rim Campground, the trail treats hikers to dramatic Canyon views and shady rambles among ponderosa pines. If you feel like stretching out your legs (but don't feel like working up a sweat) this is the trail for you. Benches are set up at several points, offering terrific views of Bright Angel Point, Bright Angel Canyon, and the many temples beyond. Along the way you'll also pass a small Ancestral Puebloan ruin. In the early morning, the Transept Trail is a great place to see wildlife such as Mule Deer, chipmunks, and squirrels. Bird watchers should keep an eye out for wrens, juncos, and woodpeckers.

TRAILHEAD   From Grand Canyon Lodge: head down the obvious trail towards Bright Angel Point and turn right off the pavement after one-tenth of a mile. From the North Rim Campground: head west from the general store and look for the sign that marks the trail.

◆ TRAIL INFO ▶

RATING: Easy

HIKING TIME: 45 minutes

DISTANCE: 3 miles, round-trip

ELEVATION CHANGE: 100 ft.

67

Fuller Canyon Road

Ken Patrick Trail

Uncle Jim Trail

Widforss Trail

Roaring Springs Canyon

North Rim
Campground

Transept Trail

Grand
Canyon
Lodge

2

Roaring
Springs

The Transept

Bright
Angel
Point

1

Oza
Butte

Widforss
Point

North Kaibab Trail

Bright Angel Canyon

∼⊲ CAPE FINAL TRAIL ⊳∼

SUMMARY This highly recommended hike heads to the easternmost tip of Walhalla Plateau, offering sweeping views of the Vishnu Temple, Jupiter Temple, and eastern Grand Canyon. The views are among the finest on the North Rim, and due to Cape Final's relatively remote location crowds are generally few and far between. From Cape Royal Road the trail heads through an open ponderosa forest, passing by several fine viewpoints. After leaving the ponderosa forest, the trail strolls past cacti and pinyon pines. Cape Final itself, reached via a faint path, can be a bit hard to find—look for the USGS datum points embedded in the bedrock at the overlook. Backpacking note: it's possible to camp at Cape Final. The park's Backcountry Office grants one camping permit per night. If you're lucky enough to get your hands on that permit, you'll have Cape Final all to yourself!

TRAILHEAD The Cape Final Trail starts along Cape Royal Road. The small trailhead (which can be easy to miss) starts roughly 11.8 miles south of the junction with Point Imperial Road (2.5 miles north of the end of Cape Royal Road).

TRAIL INFO	
RATING: Easy	**HIKING TIME:** 2 hours
DISTANCE: 4 miles, round-trip	**ELEVATION CHANGE:** 150 ft.

~ CLIFF SPRING TRAIL ~

SUMMARY This easy trail near the tip of Walhalla Plateau meanders through a forested ravine to a small spring. Not far from the start is an Ancestral Puebloan granary, used to store crops such as beans, corns, and squash in ancient times. As the trail drops down, it parallels a small creek, crossing it twice. The trail then wraps around some striking 30-foot cliffs with a pronounced overhang. Soon the small clumps of vegetation clinging to the rock walls become thick and mossy, and you can see Cliff Spring squeezing itself out of the rock. (Note: do not drink the water; it may be contaminated.) Nearby is a large flat rock where you can gaze out into the depths of the Canyon.

TRAILHEAD The Cliff Springs Trail starts on the inside of a hairpin turn about ½ mile from the end of Cape Royal Road (roughly 13.5 miles south of the junction with Point Imperial Road). Parking is available at a pullover on the left side of the road. A signed trailhead is located across the street.

TRAIL INFO

RATING: Easy

HIKING TIME: 1 hour

DISTANCE: 1 mile, round-trip

ELEVATION CHANGE: 200 ft.

Cape Final

Walhalla Plateau

Walhalla Glades Trail

Cape Royal Road

Cliff
Spring

Cape Royal

Freya
Castle

Wotans
Throne

Vishnu
Temple

~ WIDFORSS TRAIL ~

SUMMARY This long, easy hike heads deep into the forest above the Transept and ends with a fine view of the Canyon. For lovers of wildflowers and woodland scenery, the Widforss Trail has few rivals on the North Rim. The start of the trail alternates back and forth between the forest and the rim. Numbered posts corresponds to points of interest listed in a self-guiding trail brochure available at the trailhead. Among the notable sights: petrified reptile tracks (#9) and a gigantic ponderosa pine several centuries old (#10). Roughly 2.5 miles from the start the trail leaves the rim and heads through the forest, which has been burned by wildfires in places. The trail narrows towards the end, encountering a picnic table shortly before reaching stunning Widforss Point. Backpacking note: camping permits are available for the Widforss Trail.

TRAILHEAD From Grand Canyon Lodge, drive north on AZ-67 for about 2.5 miles until you see a sign for the turnoff to Widforss Point. Turn left onto the dirt road and follow it for about half a mile. There is a signed parking area for the Widforss Trail on the left. The trail starts on the south side of the parking area.

TRAIL INFO

RATING: Easy

HIKING TIME: 6 hours

DISTANCE: 10 miles, round-trip

ELEVATION CHANGE: 400 ft.

WIDFORSS TRAIL

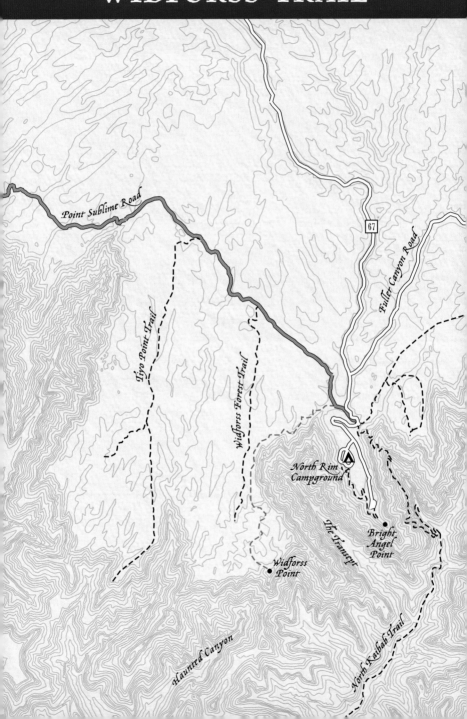

Point Sublime Road

67

Fuller Canyon Road

Tiyo Point Trail

Widforss Forest Trail

North Rim
Campground

The Transept

Bright
Angel
Point

Widforss
Point

Haunted Canyon

North Kaibab Trail

❧ NORTH KAIBAB TRAIL ❧

SUMMARY   The steep, strenuous North Kaibab Trail is the only maintained trail on the North Rim that descends into the Canyon. Though physically demanding, it offers a tremendous Inner Canyon experience, passing through a stunning range of ecological zones. Backpackers typically spend three to four days hiking the trail, spending the night at Cottonwood Campground (halfway down the trail) and Bright Angel Campground (located near the Colorado River). Day hikers can head to Coconino Overlook (1.5 miles, round-trip) or Supai Tunnel (4 miles, round-trip). Two beautiful waterfalls, Roaring Springs and Ribbon Falls, are accessible via short side trails much farther down the trail. Towards the end of the trail, you'll pass through The Box—a narrow, shady corridor that twists along Bright Angel Creek through 1.7 billion-year-old Vishnu Schist.

TRAILHEAD   The trail starts about two miles north of Grand Canyon Lodge just off AZ-67. A small parking area is located next to the trailhead. There's also a free early morning shuttle that departs from Grand Canyon Lodge (p.257).

TRAIL INFO

RATING: Strenuous

HIKING TIME: 3–4 Days

DISTANCE: 28 miles, round-trip

ELEVATION CHANGE: 5,850 ft.

NORTH KAIBAB TRAIL

Supai
Tunnel

Roaring
Springs

Bright
Angel
Point

Tiyo
Point

Widforss
Point

Cottonwood
Campground

Shiva
Temple

Manu
Temple

Ribbon
Falls

Buddha
Temple

Bright Angel Canyon

Isis
Temple

Brahma
Temple

Tower
of Set

Cheops
Pyramid

The
Box

Zoroaster
Temple

Phantom
Ranch

Bright Angel
Campground

Clear Creek Trail

Plateau
Point

Tonto Trail

Mohave
Point

Bright
Angel
Trail

Yavapai
Point

South
Kaibab
Trail

Yaki
Point

The South Rim

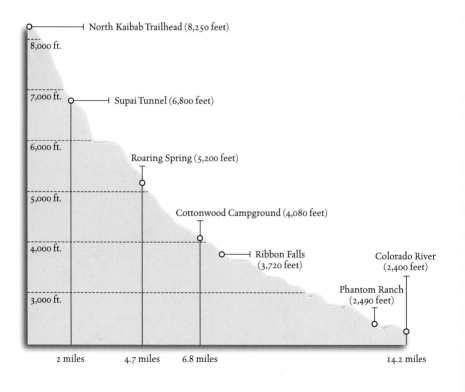

North Kaibab Trailhead (8,250 feet)

8,000 ft.

7,000 ft.   Supai Tunnel (6,800 feet)

6,000 ft.

Roaring Spring (5,200 feet)

5,000 ft.

Cottonwood Campground (4,080 feet)

4,000 ft.

Ribbon Falls
(3,720 feet)

Colorado River
(2,400 feet)

Phantom Ranch
(2,490 feet)

3,000 ft.

2 miles   4.7 miles   6.8 miles   14.2 miles

NORTH KAIBAB TRAIL

Ribbon Falls

∾∘ THUNDER RIVER FALLS ∘∾

SUMMARY The trail to Thunder River Falls is one of the most strenuous hikes in Grand Canyon, requiring physical determination and advanced backcountry skills. But if you're rugged enough to handle the challenge, it's one of the park's most rewarding hikes, blending exceptional Canyon scenery with access to several amazing sights. There are two trailheads that lead to Thunder River Falls: Monument Point and Indian Hollow. The information listed here is for Monument Point, which adds 800 feet of elevation but cuts out five miles of extra hiking. After two steep drops you'll merge with the Thunder River Trail and cross the broad Esplanade. Continue to Thunder River Falls and Tapeats Creek. Be sure to give yourself an extra day to explore Deer Creek Narrows and Deer Creek Falls—two of Grand Canyon's most beautiful sights.

TRAILHEAD From Grand Canyon Lodge drive north on AZ-67. Four miles past the park entrance station turn west onto Forest Road 22. Drive 11 miles, then turn left onto Forest Road 292. Go straight, then turn onto Forest Road 292A and drive four miles to Monument Point.

TRAIL INFO

RATING: Very Strenuous	**HIKING TIME:** 3–4 Days
DISTANCE: 24 miles, round-trip	**ELEVATION CHANGE:** 6,250 ft.

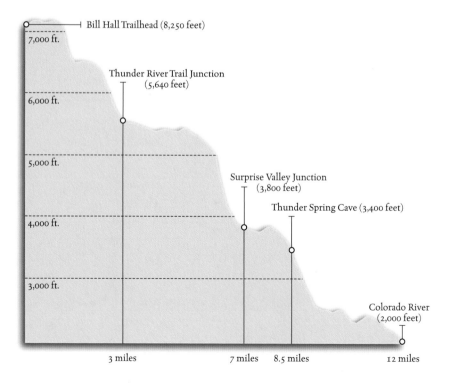

Bill Hall Trailhead (8,250 feet)

7,000 ft.

Thunder River Trail Junction
(5,640 feet)

6,000 ft.

5,000 ft.

Surprise Valley Junction
(3,800 feet)

Thunder Spring Cave (3,400 feet)

4,000 ft.

3,000 ft.

Colorado River
(2,000 feet)

3 miles   7 miles   8.5 miles   12 miles

THUNDER RIVER TRAIL

Thunder River Falls

Deer Creek Narrows

Deer Creek Narrows

HAVASU CANYON

★ ★ ★ ★ ★

Introduction 285
Basics 286
Map 288
Sights 289

HAVASU CANYON

To GRAND CANYON visitors in the know, the word *Havasu* conjures up images of a remote desert paradise. Havasu Canyon, located about 35 miles west of Grand Canyon Village, is one of the most shockingly beautiful places in the Southwest. For over 700 years it has been the home of the Havasupai Indians, the "People of the Blue-Green Water," who derive their name from the vivid turquoise stream that flows through the center of the canyon. The Havasupai Indians continue to live in the tiny village of Supai (population 450) located 2,000 feet below the rim. A short distance from the village are Havasu Falls and Mooney Falls, two of the most gorgeous waterfalls in North America.

Although Havasu Canyon only receives nine inches of rain a year, it drains a 3,000 square-mile basin, enough to create a steady stream flowing through the canyon at about 38 million gallons a day. Even more impressive, the stream tumbles down the canyon in a series of beautiful pools and waterfalls. The color of the water, an unearthly blue more typical of the Caribbean than the desert Southwest, is caused by a light coating of travertine (calcium carbonate) that reflects off the riverbed.

Is Havasu Canyon too good to be true? Almost. Due to its rugged, remote location, getting here is a bit of a challenge, requiring long drives along desolate roads and a rugged descent into the canyon by a) foot, b) mule, or c) helicopter. No roads lead to Supai, which is the last town in the United States where daily mail is still delivered by mule. Furthermore, all visitors to Havasu must obtain a permit before entering the canyon. To prevent overcrowding, the Havasupai keep the number of permits issued deliberately low at about 35,000 per year.

In many ways, Havasu Canyon feels like the land that time forgot. The Havasupai Indians still living in Supai continue to speak their native tongue, horses and dogs freely roam the dirt roads, and illumination is only provided by the sun. All this, combined with breathtaking natural scenery, makes a visit to Havasu Canyon one of the most fascinating adventures in America.

Havasu Canyon
BASICS

BASIC INFO

For the most up-to-date info regarding Havasu Canyon, check out the Havasupai Tribe's web site at www.havasupaitribe.com

GETTING TO HAVASU

Although Havasu Canyon only lies about 35 miles west of Grand Canyon Village, it's about 200 miles away by road. The trail to the village of Supai starts at the rim of Havasu Canyon at Hualapai Hilltop. To get there from Grand Canyon Village, take I-40 to the town of Seligman, then turn onto AZ-66 heading toward Peach Springs. A little under 30 miles past Seligman (six miles east of Peach Springs) turn onto Indian Route Highway 18 and follow it roughly 60 miles to Hualapai Hilltop. From the hilltop you have three options to get to Supai:

On Foot—The trail to Supai is about eight miles. Plan on roughly three hours hiking down and four hours hiking up. Despite a series of strenuous switchbacks near the top, the majority of the trail is a moderate/easy hike. To lighten your load, you can arrange to have your bag carried down by mule.

By Mule—Mule rides to Supai cost $70 per person one-way, $120 round-trip They are best booked through the lodge (928-448-2111). A ride to the campground, located past the village, can be arranged by Havasupai Tourist Enterprises (928-448-2121) for $75 one-way, $150 round-trip. One mule can also carry up to four bags weighing up to 130 pounds for the price of one rider.

By Helicopter—Papillon Helicopters offers flights from Grand Canyon Airport in Tusayan to Havasu Canyon for $535 round-trip. Included in the price is a horse ride to the waterfalls. (928-638-2419, www.papillon.com)

PERMITS & FEES

All visitors *must* have an advance reservation at either the campground or lodge prior to arrival. There's also a $35 per person entrance fee. All campers must check in and pay the fee at the tourist office in Supai, open 9am–5pm.

LODGING

A small, two-story lodge in Supai offers motel-style rooms that sleep up to four. All rooms have air conditioning and private bathrooms, but no telephones or TV. Between May and October the lodge is generally booked months in advance. **Rates**: $145 per night (928-448-2111).

CAMPING

A gorgeous 200-person campground, located two miles beyond Supai near Havasu Falls, is open year-round. Campsites are located on either side of Havasu Stream, but no fires are permitted. Reservations (928-448-2141) are usually easy to come by, except during peak summer season or on busy holiday weekends. Cost: $10 per person. (On a macabre note: the campground is located on an ancient Havasupai burial ground. In the late 1800s Congress seized much of Havasu Canyon, including the burial ground, which was later mined for lead, silver, and zinc. The land was ultimately returned to the Havasupai in 1975.)

FOOD & DINING

Supai only has one restaurant: the Tribal Cafe, which serves cafeteria-style food near Supai Lodge. Hours vary, but the cafe is generally open 6 a.m.–6 p.m. in the summer, 8 a.m.–5 p.m. in the winter (928-448-2981, cash only). There's also a small grocery store across from the Cafe that sells basic goods at steep prices.

LODGING NEAR HUALAPAI HILLTOP

Driving to Hualapai Hilltop from Grand Canyon Village or any major city takes several hours, and after a grueling drive the last thing you'll want to do is start a grueling hike down Havasu Canyon. A better option is to spend the night at one of the handful of hotels located along AZ-66, which, although at least an hour away from Hualapai Hilltop, will make for a much less stressful trip.

HUALAPAI LODGE
A modern, sixty-room hotel located in Peach Springs Rates: $90–$110. (928-769-2230, www.destinationgrandcanyon.com).

GRAND CANYON CAVERNS INN
48-room motel located next to Grand Canyon Cavern, a natural limestone cavern 210 feet underground. Rates: $65–$75 (877-422-4459, www.gccaverns.com).

HAVASU CANYON

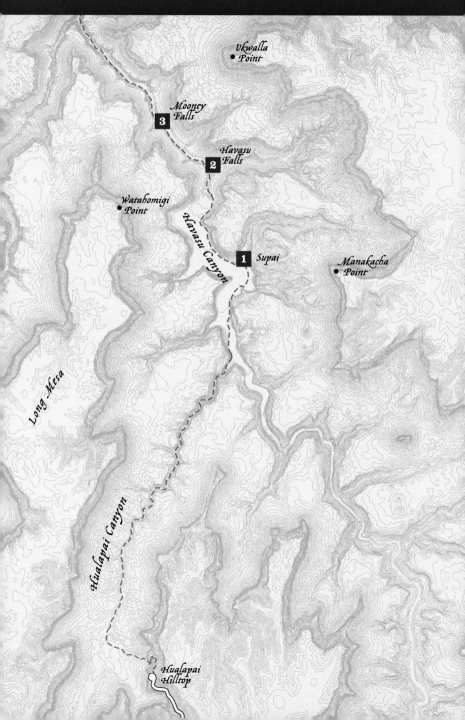

Supai Lodge

1 Supai Village

In the 1930s an anthropologist visiting Supai remarked that it was "the only spot in the United States where native culture has remained in anything like its pristine condition." Although modernization has since come to Supai in the form of electricity, telephones, and the Internet, the pace of life remains distinctly different from that of the outside world—and the Havasupai like it that way. Any suggestions to build a road into the canyon have always been heartily rejected.

The earliest residents of Havasu Canyon were an ancient culture called the Cohonina. It's unknown if the Havasupai are descendents of the Cohonina, or if they are an entirely separate group, but by A.D. 1300 the Havasupai had established themselves in Havasu canyon. They took advantage of the steady flow of water in the summer, and they moved above the rim in the winter when the tall walls of Havasu Canyon only let in about five hours of sunlight each day.

In 1776 a Spanish missionary named Francisco Thomás Garcés became the first white man to set eyes on Havasu Canyon. Several decades later, American prospectors arrived in search of gold. Then, in 1866, Congress granted much of the Havasupai's traditional lands to the Atlantic and Pacific Railroad, and the Havasupai were forced onto a reservation in Havasu Canyon less than one square mile in size. Finally in 1975, after much legal wrangling, the Havasupai Reservation was expanded to its present size of 185,000 acres.

② Havasu Falls

Havasu Falls, Havasu Canyon's star attraction, is located about two miles past the village of Supai. To get there, follow Supai's main road down the canyon until it turns into a dirt path. After 1.5 miles you'll reach Navajo Falls, a series of steep cascades tumbling down an overgrown cliff. Continue along the path for another half mile to reach Havasu Falls. As the trail starts to descend along the western canyon wall, Havasu Falls makes a sudden, spectacular appearance to your right. At this point you're at eye level with the top of the 100-foot falls. Continue down the trail to reach several well-trodden side trails that lead to a beach area. Although crowded in the summer, the beach is without question one of the most spectacular swimming holes in America.

A century ago Havasu Falls was a much different waterfall than the one you see today. Back then the waterfall cascaded over the cliff in a wide curtain of water. Then, several decades ago, a flash flood roared through Havasu Canyon and knocked out a large notch in the cliff. Suddenly, the creek was channeled into a much narrower—and much more spectacular—waterfall. Other flash floods have been much less kind. In 1993 a flash flood destroyed several beautiful travertine terraces at the base of the falls that formed a series of cascading pools. Today, brand new terraces are slowly rebuilding.

Note: Because Havasu Canyon drains such a vast area, flash floods are a constant threat. See page 23 for more on flash floods.

③ Mooney Falls

Mooney Falls is the tallest waterfall in Havasu Canyon. At 196 feet, it's taller than Niagara Falls. To get there, follow the main path one mile past Havasu Falls to a stunning overlook. To reach the base of the falls, you'll have to descend a series of slippery ladders and steps that are not for the faint of heart. Use caution if you follow this route. Although the trail continues past the base of Mooney Falls, it becomes quite rugged as it descends farther down the canyon.

The Havasupai call Mooney Falls "Mother of the Waters", and they consider it to be their most sacred waterfall. The name Mooney Falls comes from a tragic accident that occurred here in 1880. In that year a group of American prospectors descended Havasu Canyon in the hopes of finding gold, but when they reached this waterfall they could go no farther. The Havasupai Indians told the prospectors that no man had ever passed beyond the waterfall, only the "birds of the air or spirits of the dead." Undeterred, a man named Daniel Mooney asked to be lowered down by rope. With a rope tied around his waist, a group of miners and Havasupai lowered him over the falls. But during his descent the rope became stuck in a jagged crevice. As the men struggled to free the rope, it began to fray. The rope then snapped, and Mooney fell to his death. Unable to reach their friend, the remaining prospectors were forced to return 10 months later and build a ladder to the base of the falls. By the time they reached Mooney's body, it was encrusted in a fresh layer of travertine, and he was buried where he lay.

Mooney Falls

Ancestral Puebloans 69
Backcountry Hikes 20
Backcountry Office 21
Backcountry Permits 21
Bass, Bill 89
Beaver Falls 240
Best Western Inn 118
Bighorn Sheep 50
Blacktail Canyon 233
Bobcats 52
Boucher, Louis 154
Bright Angel Campground 114
Bright Angel Lodge 112, 133
Bright Angel Point 259
Bright Angel Trail 172
Brower, David 100, 101
Bus Tours, South Rim 116
California Condor 54
Cameron, Ralph 94
Camping, Havasu 287
Camping, North Rim 256
Camping, South Rim 114
Canyon View Info Plaza 124
Cape Final Trail 266
Cape Royal 262
Carbon Canyon 222
Cibola, Seven Cities of 75
Cliff Spring Trail 268
Colorado Plateau 38
Colorado River 199
Colorado River Compact 211
Colorado River Trips 27
Colter, Mary 128
Coronado 75
Day Hikes 20
Debris Flows 23
Deer Creek Falls 234
Deer Creek Narrows 280
Desert View 170
Desert View Campground 114
Devils Corkscrew 176
Dining, North Rim 256
Dining, South Rim 116

Dining, Tusayan 119
Dominy, Floyd 100
Dory 29
Ecology 43
Elk 56
El Tovar Dining Room 116
El Tovar Hotel 113, 130
Elves Chasm 232
Flash Floods 23
Flights, Scenic 31
Geology 33
Glen Canyon Dam 214
Grand Canyon Airport 110
Grand Canyon Camper Village 119
Grand Canyon Caverns Inn 287
Grand Canyon Lodge 256, 260
Grand Canyon Music Festival 117
Grand Canyon Quality Inn 118
Grand Canyon Trailway 110
Grand Hotel 118
Grandview Point 162
Grandview Trail 192
Great Unconformity 34
Hance, John 88
Havasu Canyon 239, 285
Havasupai 73
Helicopter Flights 31
Hermits Rest 154
Hermit Trail 186
Hiking 19
Holiday Inn 119
Hopi 72
Hopi House 128
Hopi Point 146
Hualapai 73
Hualapai Hilltop 286
Hualapai Lodge 287
Humpback Chub 66
Ice Age 46
IMAX Theater 119
Indian Garden Campground 114
Introduction 9
Kachina Lodge 113

Kanab Canyon 236
Kolb Studio 138
Lava Falls 247
Lee, John D. 89
Lees Ferry 216
Lipan Point 168
Lodging, Havasu 287
Lodging, North Rim 256
Lodging, South Rim 112
Lodging, Tusyan 118
Lookout Studio 137
Marble Canyon 218
Maricopa Point 142
Maswik Lodge 113
Mather Campground 114
Mather Point 122
Matkatamiba Canyon 244
Mohave Point 150
Moran Point 166
Mountain Lions 58
Mule Deer 60
Mule Trips 25
Nankoweap 224
National Canyon 242
Navajo 73
North Kaibab Trail 272
North Rim 253
North Rim Campground 256
North Rim General Store 257
Owens, Uncle Jim 92
Permits, Hiking 21
Pet Kennel 117
Pima Point 152
Plateau Point 179
Point Imperial 262
Powell, John Wesley 79
Powell Point 145
Railroad 91
Rainbow Trout 67
Ralph Cameron 94
Ranger Programs, North Rim 257
Ranger Programs, South Rim 116
Rattlesnakes 64

Red Feather Lodge 119
Redwall Cavern 221
Restaurants, North Rim 256
Restaurants, South Rim 116
Restaurants, Tusayan 119
Ribbon Falls 275
Rim to Rim Shuttle 254
River Outfitters 28
River Trips 27
Roosevelt, Teddy 97
Saddle Canyon 223
Santa Fe Train Depot 136
Scenic Flights 31
Shinumo Creek 229
Shuttle, South Rim 115
Southern Paiute 72
South Kaibab Trail 180
South Rim 107
Supai Campground 287
Supai Lodge 287
Ten X Campground 119
The Guide 111
Thunderbird Lodge 113
Thunder River Falls 276
Trailer Village 114
Transept Trail 264
Trinity Canyon 228
Tusayan 118
Tusayan Ruin 167
Vishnu Temple 161
Walhalla Plateau 262
Weather, 45
Weather, South Rim 112
Weather, North Rim 255
White, James 79
Widforss Trail 270
Yaki Point 158
Yavapai Point 127
Zoroaster Temple 149

The Best of the Best

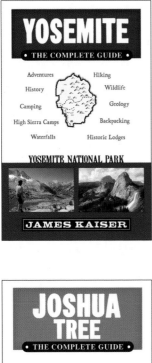

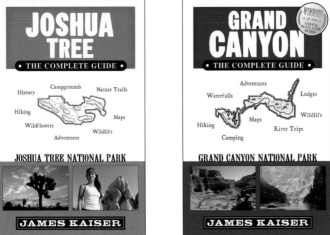

www.jameskaiser.com